WRITING JAPANESE HIRAGANA

An Introductory Japanese Language Workbook

JIM GLEESON

TUTTLE Publishing

Tokyo | Rutland, Vermont | Singapore

"Books to Span the East and West"

Tuttle Publishing was founded in 1832 in the small New England town of Rutland, Vermont [USA]. Our core values remain as strong today as they were then—to publish best-in-class books which bring people together one page at a time. In 1948, we established a publishing outpost in Japan—and Tuttle is now a leader in publishing English-language books about the arts, languages and cultures of Asia. The world has become a much smaller place today and Asia's economic and cultural influence has grown. Yet the need for meaningful dialogue and information about this diverse region has never been greater. Over the past seven decades, Tuttle has published thousands of books on subjects ranging from martial arts and paper crafts to language learning and literature—and our talented authors, illustrators, designers and photographers have won many prestigious awards. We welcome you to explore the wealth of information available on Asia at www.tuttlepublishing.com.

Published by Tuttle Publishing, an imprint of Periplus Editions (HK) Ltd.

www.tuttlepublishing.com

Text © 1996, 2015 Jim Gleeson

LCC Card No. 2004105695
ISBN 978-4-8053-1349-7
This edition first published, 2015

This title was first published in 1996 as *Introduction to Written Japanese Hiragana*.

28 27 26 25 24
13 12 11 10 9   2408VP
Printed in Malaysia

TUTTLE PUBLISHING® is a registered trademark of Tuttle Publishing, a division of Periplus Editions (HK) Ltd.

Distributed by:

Japan
Tuttle Publishing
Yaekari Building, 3rd Floor
5-4-12 Osaki, Shinagawa-ku
Tokyo 141 0032
Tel: (81) 3 5437-0171
Fax: (81) 3 5437-0755
sales@tuttle.co.jp
www.tuttle.co.jp

North America, Latin America & Europe
Tuttle Publishing
364 Innovation Drive
North Clarendon,
VT 05759-9436 U.S.A.
Tel: 1 (802) 773-8930
Fax: 1 (802) 773-6993
info@tuttlepublishing.com
www.tuttlepublishing.com

Asia Pacific
Berkeley Books Pte. Ltd.
3 Kallang Sector #04-01
Singapore 349278
Tel: (65) 6741-2178
Fax: (65) 6741-2179
inquiries@periplus.com.sg
www.tuttlepublishing.com

はじめに

It is widely accepted that students of Japanese progress more quickly if they learn the written component of the language at an early stage of their studies. Unfortunately, many students are daunted by the task of learning a large number of seemingly complex characters.

The complexity of Japanese characters, however, is something of an illusion, for many of the characters are merely combinations of comparatively few elements. This fact becomes apparent as one progresses through the two forty-eight character syllabaries, known collectively as kana, and the two thousand or so kanji characters that are used in written Japanese today.

Anybody who is able to master English, with its irregular spellings and idiosyncratic pronunciations, is more than equipped to master written Japanese.

The hiragana and katakana syllabaries are purely phonetic characters, which function much like the letters of the English alphabet. In this respect, kana are quite different from kanji characters, which are based on Chinese ideographs. The basic function of hiragana is to supplement the kanji.

Generally, kanji are used to represent the ideas in a sentence while hiragana is used to represent the relationships between the ideas. For example, whereas the concept of 'go' would be written in kanji, hiragana would be suffixed to the kanji to indicate "want to go," "went," "will not go," and so forth. Hiragana is also used for particles such as "to," "in," "by" and "at."

Each of the hiragana and katakana syllabaries represents all of the sounds in spoken Japanese. Unlike kanji, which can take on a variety of pronunciations according to their context, the pronunciation of the kana characters is quite regular. Although it is possible to write Japanese using only hiragana, a native Japanese speaker would find it somewhat difficult to understand. Kanji are used for clarity, eloquence, and immediacy of meaning. It is customary for the student to write using only hiragana at first, then to substitute kanji into their writing as each character is learned.

Japanese schoolchildren learn their characters by writing them out, and this is generally acknowledged as the fastest way to master them.

This book has been prepared so that students at the introductory level of Japanese can become acquainted with the written component of the language in the quickest possible way. The overriding priority has been given to active student involvement, with a variety of practice sentences and expressions provided to reinforce the characters learned at each stage of progress. The book also features grayed-out, trace-over characters to enable the student to gain the correct feel and balance of each character.

To avoid repetition, this book uses the dictionary form of verbs rather than the ~*masu* form. In the majority of situations, however, it is customary to write using the ~*masu* form.

This book uses the Hepburn system of romanization. It is important to remember, however, that Japanese is a separate language with an independent set of sounds to English, and hence, any attempt to romanize it can only be an approximation.

■ Contents ■

もくじ

つかいかた

In both printed and handwritten Japanese, the characters occupy imaginary squares of equal size, with each character centered within its square.

All of the writing practice in this book involves writing characters within squares, and the squares have centerlines to provide the correct balance and feel for writing Japanese.

Traditionally, Japanese is written with a brush or *fude*, and this fact is reflected in many typographic styles today. Although the *fude* is no longer widely used, some principles of using a *fude* still apply to writing Japanese with a pencil or biro — in particular, the stroke endings.

The strokes of Japanese characters terminate in one of three ways, as illustrated below.

i) Jumping, to produce a hook at the end of the stroke. This ending is called *hane*, from the verb *haneru*, to jump.
ii) Bringing the pen or pencil to a stop while it is on the page. This ending is called *tome*, from the verb *tomeru*, to stop.
iii) Lifting the pen or pencil off the page while it is moving. This ending is called *harai*, meaning 'sweep.'

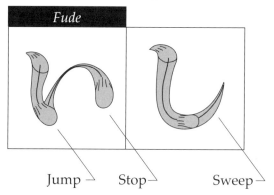

Fude

Jump ⌐ Stop ⌐   Sweep ⌐

When tracing over the characters, be sure to keep these three types of stroke endings in mind, observing how the strokes of the gray-tinted characters terminate.

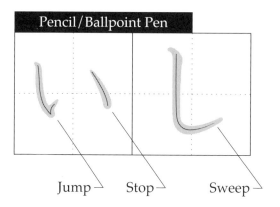

Pencil/Ballpoint Pen

Jump ⌐ Stop ⌐   Sweep ⌐

In Japanese, as in English, there are many differences between handwritten and typeset characters. To enable students to gain the correct feel for written Japanese, educators in Japan have developed a neutral typeface which incorporates the features of handwritten Japanese without the stylistic idiosyncracies of any individual.

This typeface is known simply as Schoolbook or *kyōkasho*, and is the standard typeface used to teach Japanese schoolchildren the written language. All of the practice characters in this book are set in *kyōkasho*.

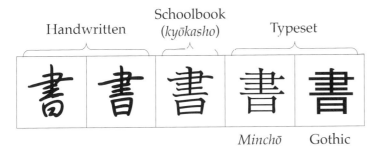

To provide familiarity with a range of type variations, each character entry in this book is accompanied by four different character styles, as shown below. These variations are included for recognition only.

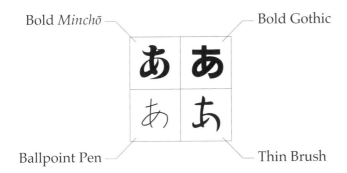

The upper left variation is a bold *Minchō* typeface while the upper right variation is a bold Gothic typeface. Typefaces of this kind are frequently used in advertisements and newspaper headlines.

The lower left typeface simulates the characters written with a ballpoint pen, while the lower right typeface is a thin brush script indicative of that used on traditional occasions.

In around 100 A.D., Chinese characters, known as kanji, entered Japan via the Korean peninsula. Since that time, many thousands of kanji have come to Japan, many of them falling into disuse or becoming obsolete. Today, there are about two thousand kanji in general use, with several thousand more being used on special or formal occasions.

Although kanji refer to ideas or objects, by around 800 A.D., a special set of kanji had evolved which were used for their pronunciation, with the innate meaning of the characters being discarded.

In the Heian period (794–1185), these characters underwent a series of simplifications and reductions via calligraphy, which was widely practiced by the aristocracy.

The result was a simple, cursive set of characters known as hiragana. Unlike kanji, which refer to ideas or objects and which can take on a variety of pronunciations according to their context, each hiragana character is pronounced in only one way, and there is no conceptual meaning.

A chart showing the evolution of all the hiragana characters is given inside the back cover.

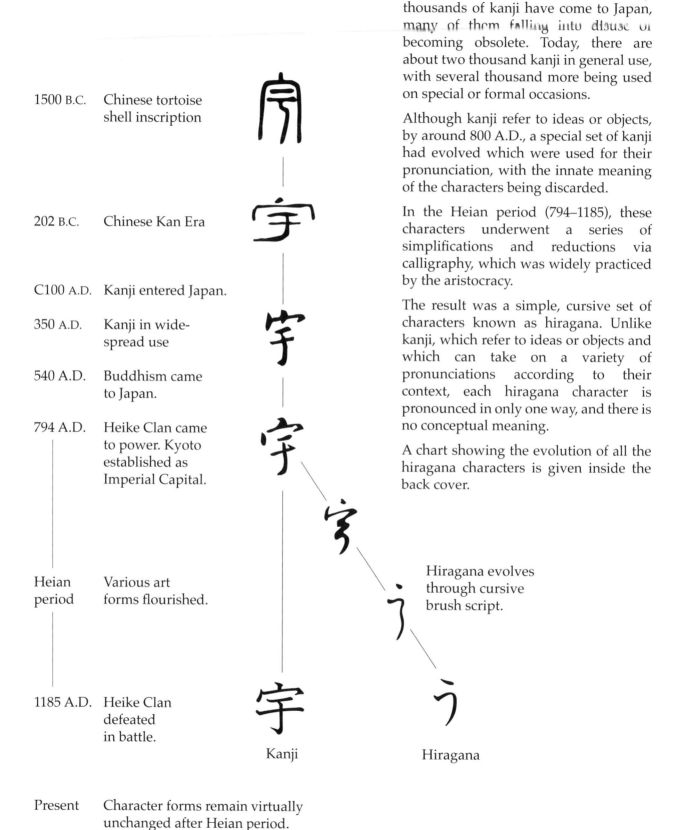

1500 B.C.	Chinese tortoise shell inscription
202 B.C.	Chinese Kan Era
C100 A.D.	Kanji entered Japan.
350 A.D.	Kanji in wide-spread use
540 A.D.	Buddhism came to Japan.
794 A.D.	Heike Clan came to power. Kyoto established as Imperial Capital.
Heian period	Various art forms flourished.
1185 A.D.	Heike Clan defeated in battle.

Hiragana evolves through cursive brush script.

Kanji   Hiragana

Present	Character forms remain virtually unchanged after Heian period.

ひらがな

a	i	u	e	o
あ	い	う	え	お

ka	ki	ku	ke	ko
か	き	く	け	こ

sa	shi	su	se	so
さ	し	す	せ	そ

ta	chi	tsu	te	to
た	ち	つ	て	と

na	ni	nu	ne	no
な	に	ぬ	ね	の

ha	hi	fu	he	ho
は	ひ	ふ	へ	ほ

ma	mi	mu	me	mo
ま	み	む	め	も

ya		yu		yo
や		ゆ		よ

ra	ri	ru	re	ro
ら	り	る	れ	ろ

wa		o		n
わ		を		ん

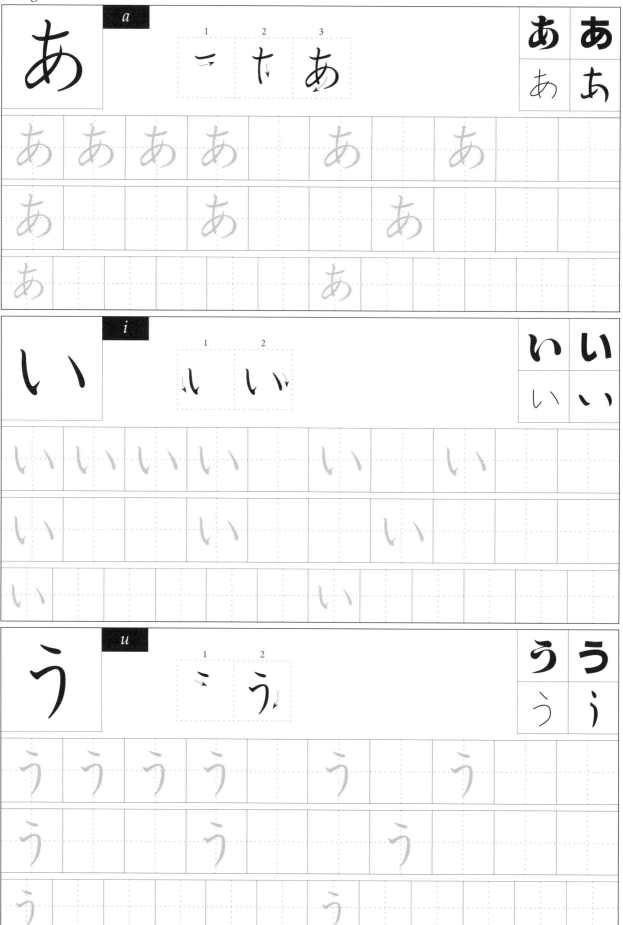

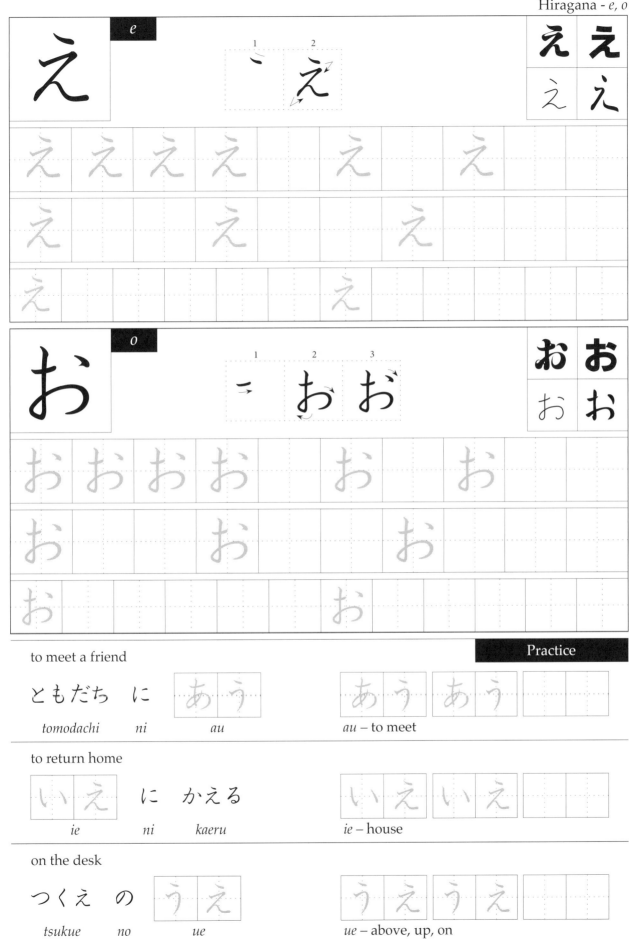

え

Practice

to meet a friend

ともだち に　あう

tomodachi　*ni*　*au*

au – to meet

to return home

いえ　に　かえる

ie　*ni*　*kaeru*

ie – house

on the desk

つくえ の　うえ

tsukue　*no*　*ue*

ue – above, up, on

11

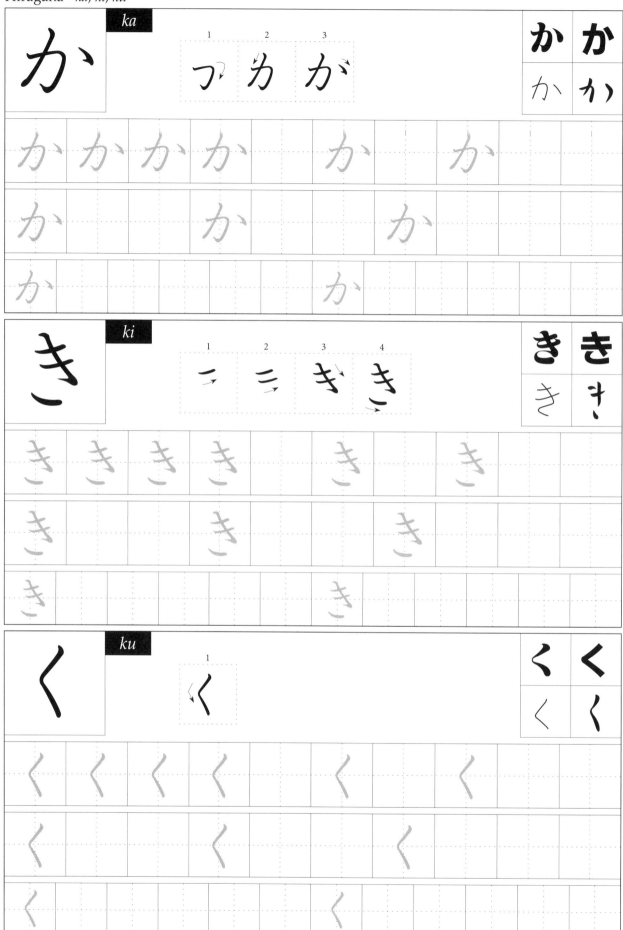

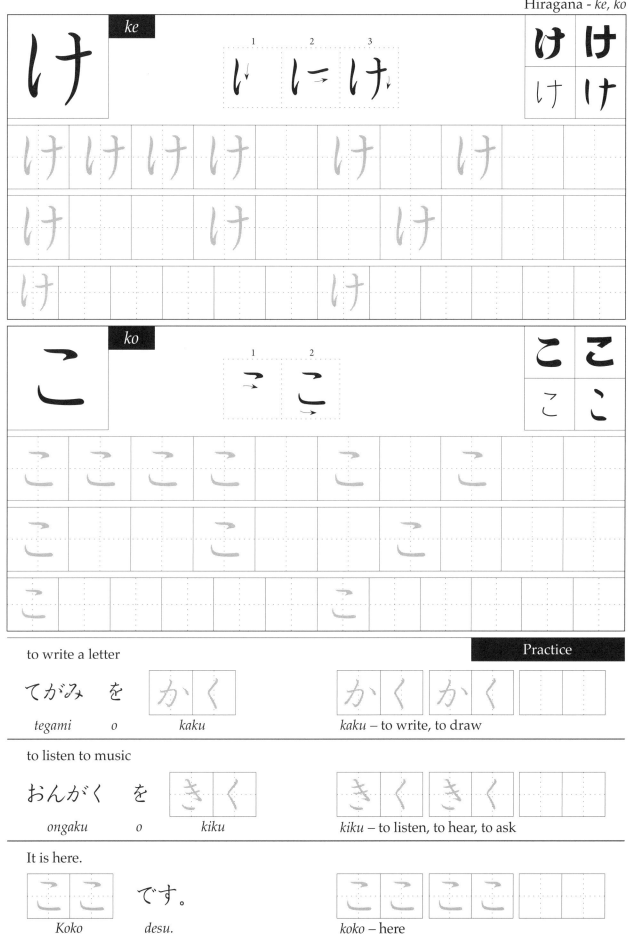

Practice

to write a letter

てがみ　を

tegami　　*o*　　*kaku*

kaku – to write, to draw

to listen to music

おんがく　を

ongaku　　*o*　　*kiku*

kiku – to listen, to hear, to ask

It is here.

です。

Koko　　*desu.*

koko – here

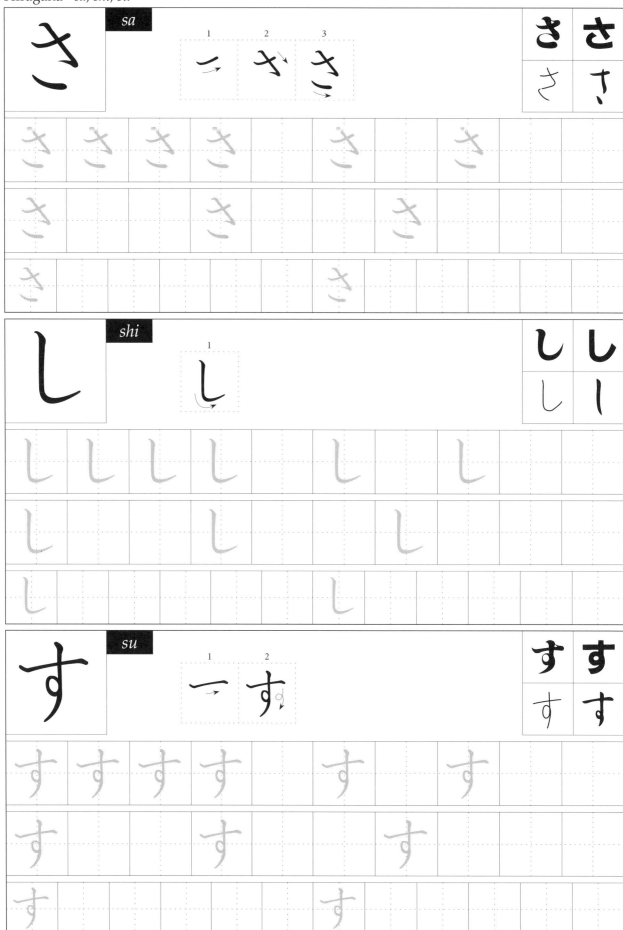

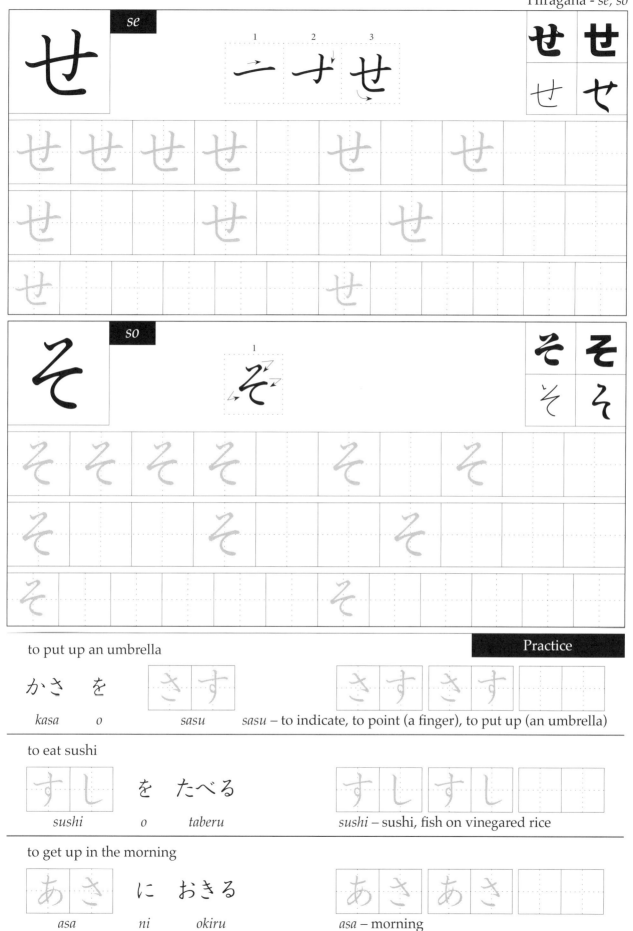

se

ニ　ナ　せ

せ せ せ せ せ せ
せ せ せ
せ せ

so

そ

そ そ そ そ そ そ
そ そ そ
そ そ

to put up an umbrella

かさ　を　さす　さす さす

kasa　*o*　*sasu*　　*sasu* – to indicate, to point (a finger), to put up (an umbrella)

to eat sushi

すし　を　たべる　すし すし

sushi　*o*　*taberu*　　*sushi* – sushi, fish on vinegared rice

to get up in the morning

あさ　に　おきる　あさ あさ

asa　*ni*　*okiru*　　*asa* – morning

I speak loudly.

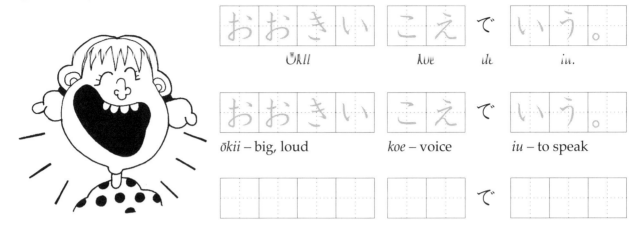

おおきい こえ で いう。
Ōkii koe de iu.

おおきい こえ で いう。

ōkii – big, loud　　　*koe* – voice　　　*iu* – to speak

［　　　　］ ［　　　］ で ［　　　］

Akiko is good natured.

あきこ は せいかく が いい。
Akiko wa seikaku ga ii.

あきこ は せいかく が いい。

Akiko – girl's name　　*seikaku* – character, nature　　*ii* – good

［　　　］ は ［　　　　］ が ［　　　］

The squid has lots of legs.

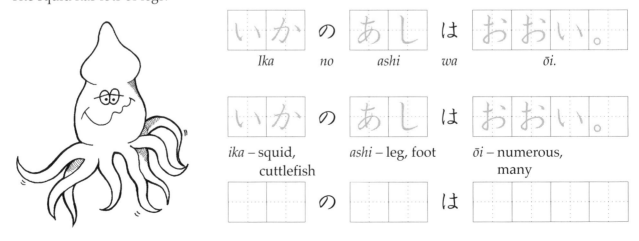

いか の あし は おおい。
Ika no ashi wa ōi.

いか の あし は おおい。

ika – squid,　　　*ashi* – leg, foot　　　*ōi* – numerous,
cuttlefish　　　　　　　　　　　　　　　　many

［　　　］ の ［　　　］ は ［　　　　］

I like delicious sushi and sake.

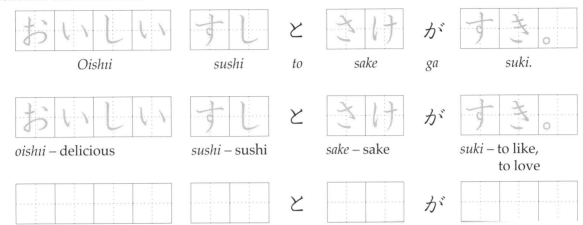

おいしい　すし　と　さけ　が　すき。

Oishii　*sushi*　*to*　*sake*　*ga*　*suki.*

おいしい　すし　と　さけ　が　すき。

oishii – delicious　*sushi* – sushi　*sake* – sake　*suki* – to like, to love

と　　が

I'll go swimming tomorrow.

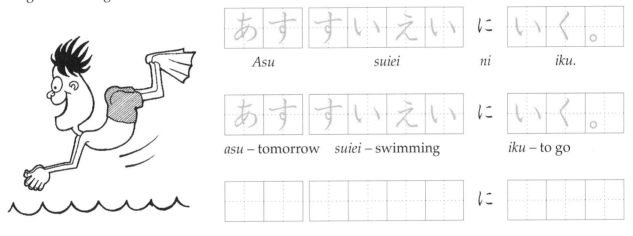

あす　すいえい　に　いく。

Asu　*suiei*　*ni*　*iku.*

あす　すいえい　に　いく。

asu – tomorrow　*suiei* – swimming　*iku* – to go

に

Asako is a slow runner.

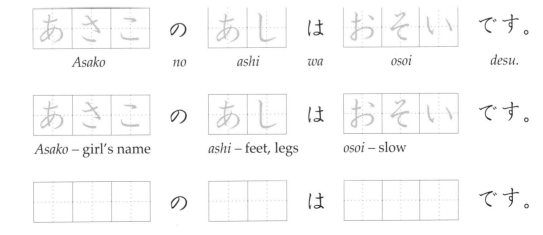

あさこ　の　あし　は　おそい　です。

Asako　*no*　*ashi*　*wa*　*osoi*　*desu.*

あさこ　の　あし　は　おそい　です。

Asako – girl's name　*ashi* – feet, legs　*osoi* – slow

の　　は　　です。

I'll buy sake at the international airport.

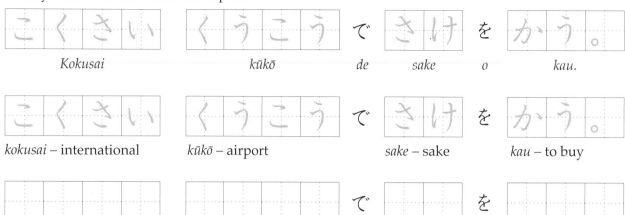

こくさい | くうこう | で | さけ | を | かう。
Kokusai | *kūkō* | *de* | *sake* | *o* | *kau.*

こくさい | くうこう | で | さけ | を | かう。
kokusai – international | *kūkō* – airport | *sake* – sake | *kau* – to buy

で | を

The cow eats the grass.

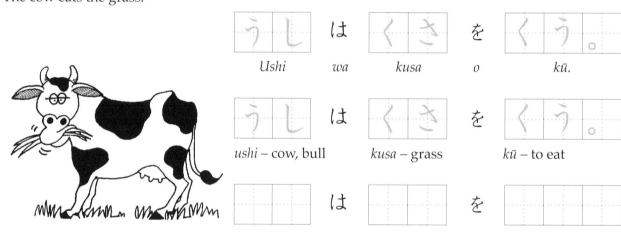

うし | は | くさ | を | くう。
Ushi | *wa* | *kusa* | *o* | *kū.*

うし | は | くさ | を | くう。
ushi – cow, bull | *kusa* – grass | *kū* – to eat

は | を

I prefer the autumn climate in Osaka.

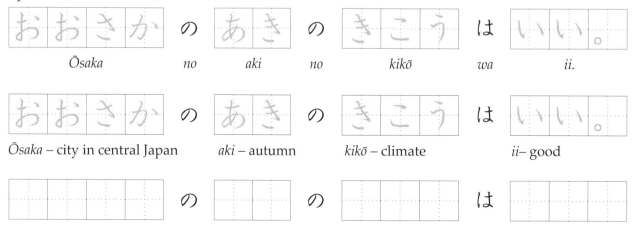

おおさか | の | あき | の | きこう | は | いい。
Ōsaka | *no* | *aki* | *no* | *kikō* | *wa* | *ii.*

おおさか | の | あき | の | きこう | は | いい。
Ōsaka – city in central Japan | *aki* – autumn | *kikō* – climate | *ii* – good

の | の | は

I'll put the chair over there.

あそこ　に　いす　を　おく。
Asoko ni isu o oku.

あそこ　に　いす　を　おく。

asoko – over there　　*isu* – chair　　*oku* – to put, to place

___ に ___ を ___

I'll draw the square accurately.

しかく　を　せいかく　に　かく。
Shikaku o seikaku ni kaku.

しかく　を　せいかく　に　かく。

shikaku – square　　*seikaku* – accuracy　　*kaku* – to write, to draw

___ を ___ に ___

I'll buy some candy at the station.

えき　で　おかし　を　かう。
Eki de okashi o kau.

えき　で　おかし　を　かう。

eki – station　　*okashi* – sweets, candy　　*kau* – to buy

___ で ___ を ___

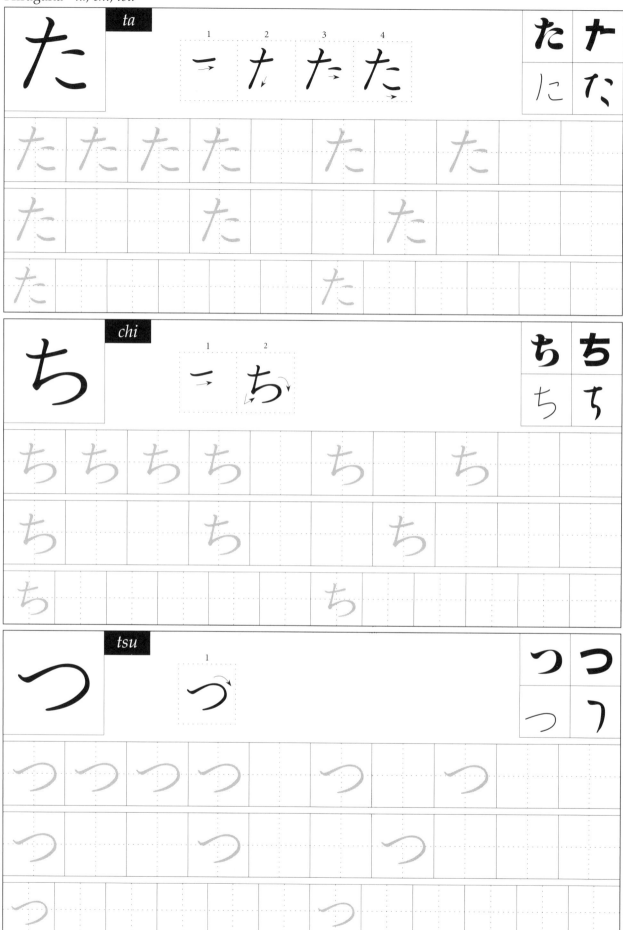

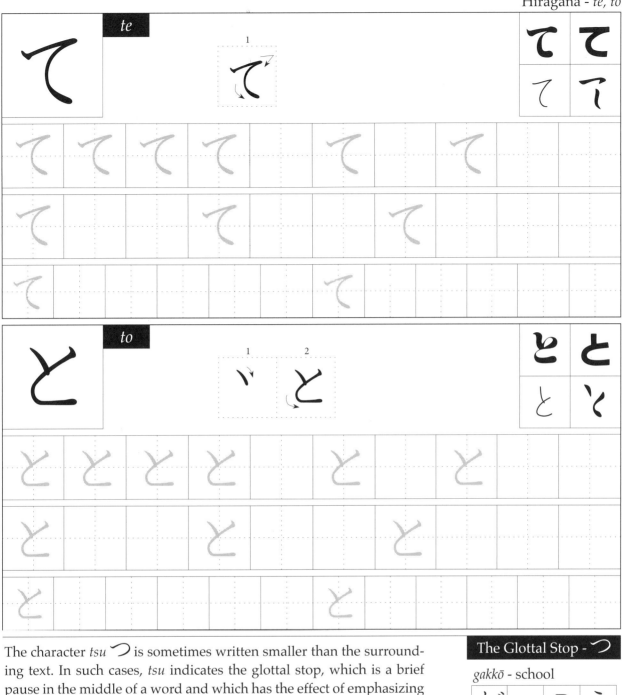

The character *tsu* つ is sometimes written smaller than the surrounding text. In such cases, *tsu* indicates the glottal stop, which is a brief pause in the middle of a word and which has the effect of emphasizing the subsequent constant. A glottal stop is romanized by doubling the subsequent character.

The Glottal Stop - つ

gakkō - school

Practice

to stand next to the chair

いす　の　となり　に　

isu　　*no*　*tonari*　*ni*　　　*tatsu*

tatsu – to stand, to rise

It is dirty.

　が　ついている。

Tsuchi　　　*ga*　　*tsuite iru.*

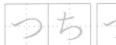　

tsuchi – earth, soil, the ground

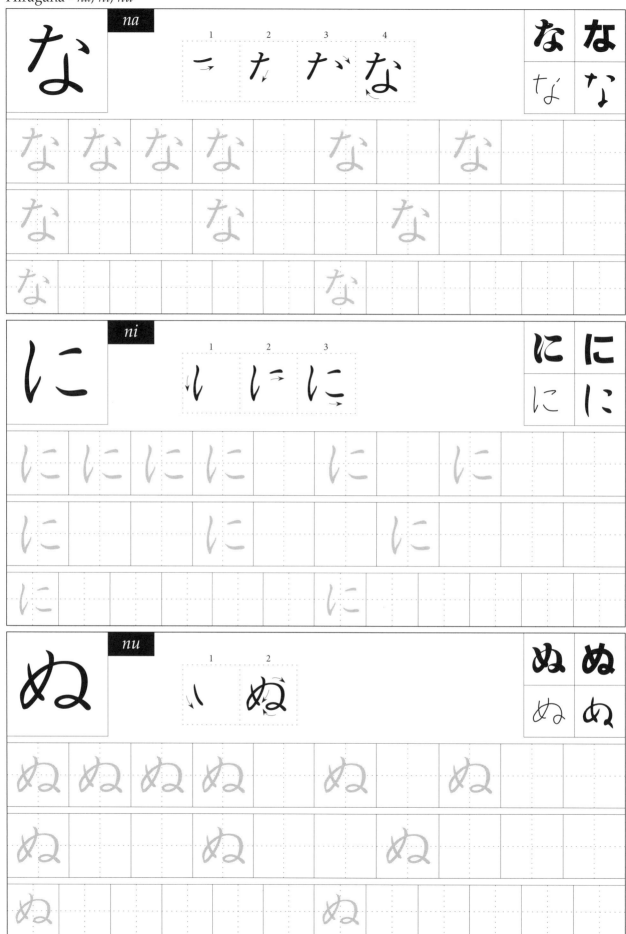

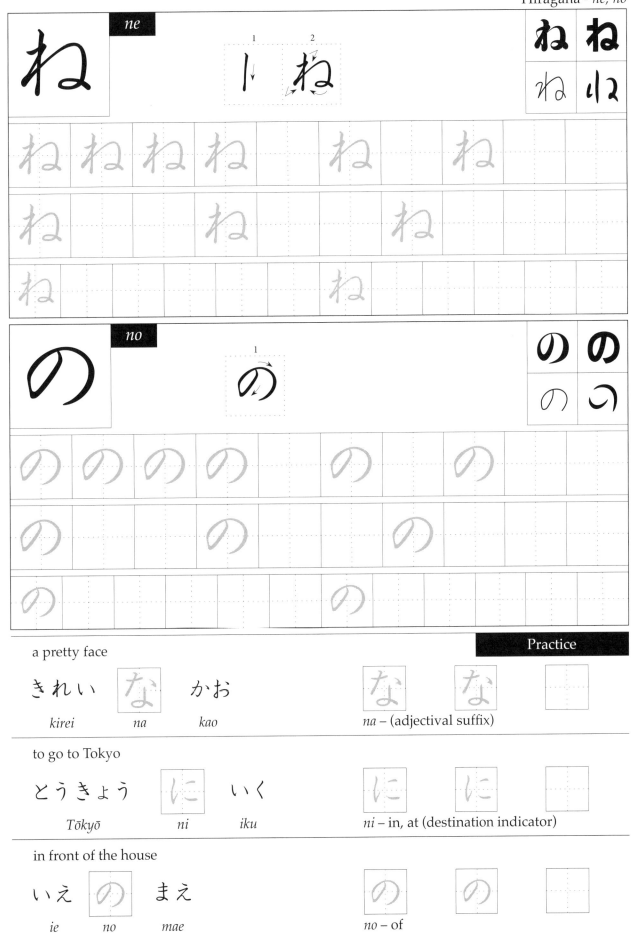

Practice

a pretty face

きれい な かお

kirei *na* *kao*

な な

na – (adjectival suffix)

to go to Tokyo

とうきょう に いく

Tōkyō *ni* *iku*

に に

ni – in, at (destination indicator)

in front of the house

いえ の まえ

ie *no* *mae*

の の

no – of

23

は **ha***

1 2 3

* Pronounced '*wa*' when indicating the subject of a sentence.

ひ **hi**

1

ふ **fu**

1 2 3 4

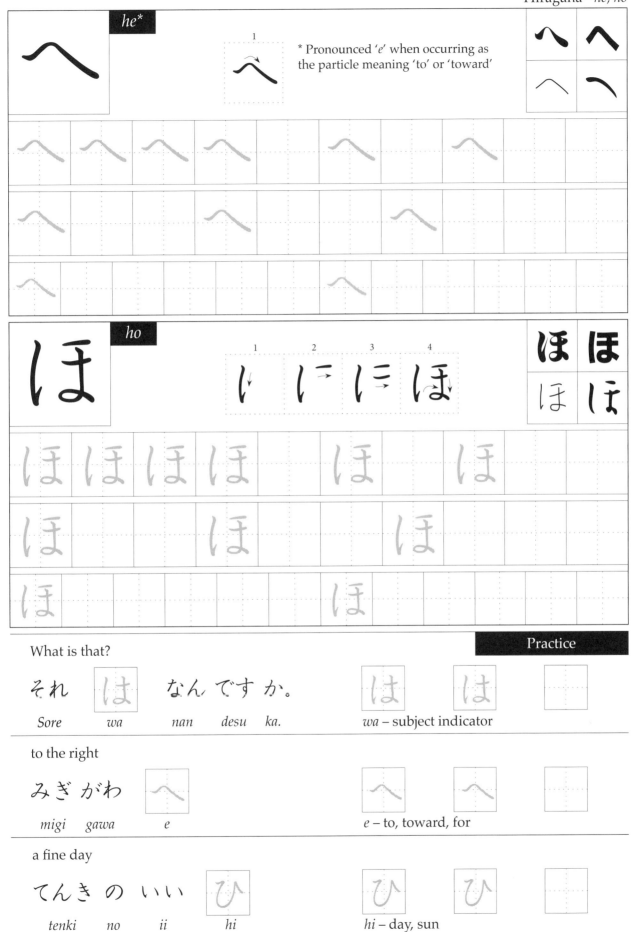

he*

* Pronounced '*e*' when occurring as the particle meaning 'to' or 'toward'

ho

Practice

What is that?

それ　は　なん　です　か。

Sore　wa　nan　desu　ka.

wa – subject indicator

to the right

みぎ がわ へ

migi gawa e

e – to, toward, for

a fine day

てんき の いい ひ

tenki no ii hi

hi – day, sun

A tall person

せ が たかい ひと
se *ga* *takai* *hito*

せ が たかい ひと

se – height, stature   *takai* – tall, high, expensive   *hito* – person

が

I'm moving to Fukuoka this year.

こ と し ふ く お か に ひっこし する。
Kotoshi   *Fukuoka*   *ni*   *hikkoshi*   *suru.*

こ と し ふ く お か に ひっこし する。

kotoshi – this year   *Fukuoka* – a city in western Japan   *hikkoshi suru* – to relocate

---

Fat legs, skinny legs

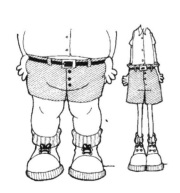

ふ と い あ し 、 ほ そ い あ し
futoi   *ashi*   *hosoi*   *ashi*

ふ と い あ し 、 ほ そ い あ し

futoi – large in diameter   *ashi* – leg, foot   *hosoi* – small in diameter

The first of the month is the day after tomorrow.

  です。

Tsuitachi   *wa*   *asatte*   *desu.*

  です。

tsuitachi – the first of the month   *asatte* – the day after tomorrow

です。

I beat a red drum.

  を

Akai   *taiko*   *o*   *tataku.*

  を

akai – red   *taiko* – drum   *tataku* – to beat, to hit

を

You are holding your chopsticks the wrong way.

  が

Hashi   *no*   *tsukaikata*   *ga*   *okashii.*

  が

hashi – chopsticks   *tsukau/tsukaikata* – to use / style of using   *okashii* – funny, strange

が

That person is stylish, isn't she?

あの	ひとは	かっこいい	です	ね。
Ano	hito wa	kakkoii	desu	ne

ano – that   *hito* – person   *kakkoii* – good appearance   *ne* – isn't she / aren't they, etc.

です

A short person

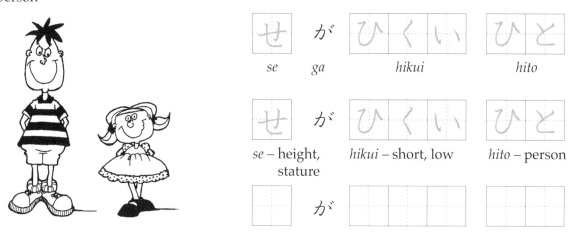

せ	が	ひくい	ひと
se	ga	hikui	hito

se – height, stature   *hikui* – short, low   *hito* – person

が

It's better if you go this way.

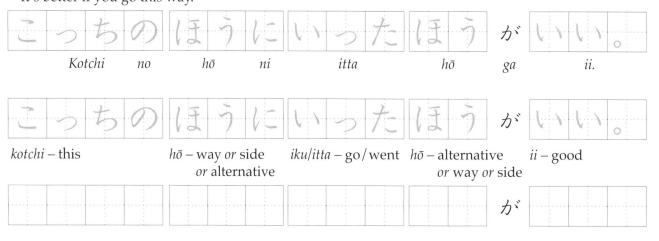

こっちの	ほうに	いった	ほう	が	いい。
Kotchi no	hō ni	itta	hō	ga	ii.

kotchi – this   *hō* – way *or* side *or* alternative   *iku/itta* – go/went   *hō* – alternative *or* way *or* side   *ii* – good

が

A small airplane

chiisa-na

hikōki

chiisa-na – small

hikōki – airplane

Takashi is very good at gymnastics.

  が  です。

Takashi *wa* *taisō* *ga* *tokui* *desu.*

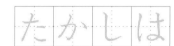  が  です。

Takashi – boy's name *taisō* – gymnastics *tokui* – one's strong point

が　　　　　です。

A cat in a box

hako *no* *naka* *no* *neko*

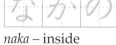 

hako – box *naka* – inside *neko* – cat

29

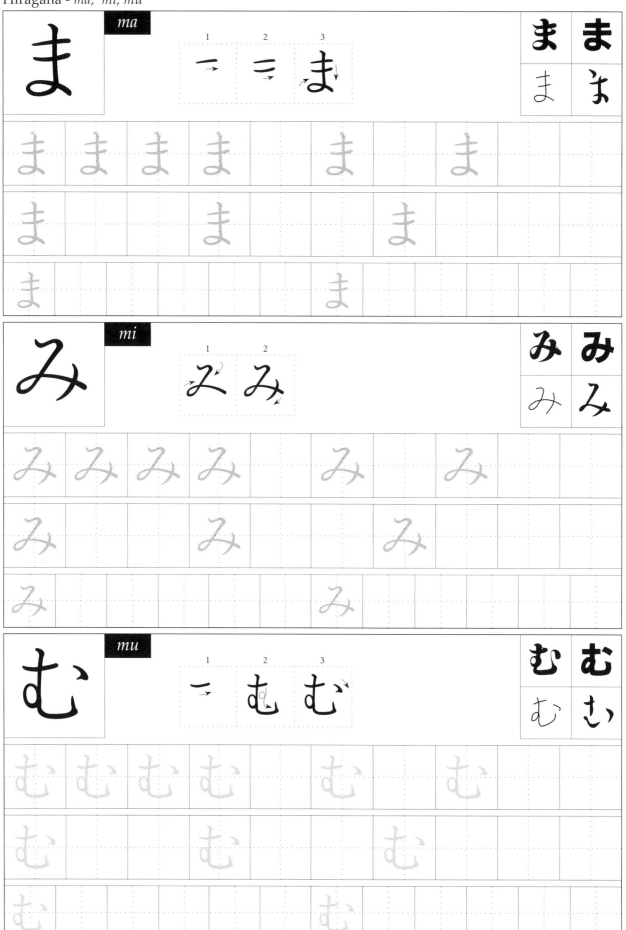

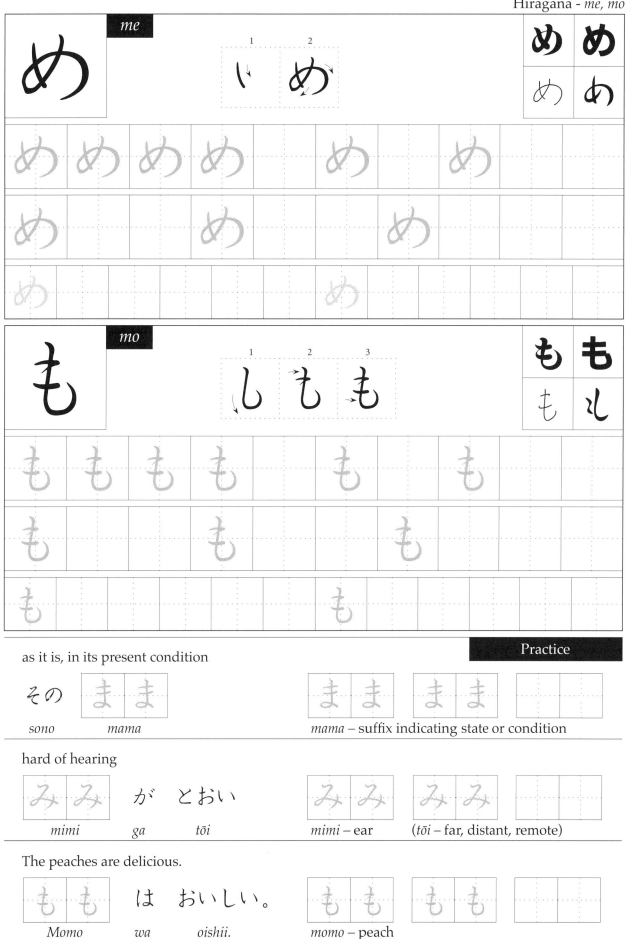

me

mo

Practice

as it is, in its present condition

その ま ま ま ま ま ま

sono   *mama*   *mama* – suffix indicating state or condition

hard of hearing

み み が とおい み み み み

mimi   *ga*   *tōi*   *mimi* – ear   (*tōi* – far, distant, remote)

The peaches are delicious.

も も は おいしい。 も も も も

Momo   *wa*   *oishii.*   *momo* – peach

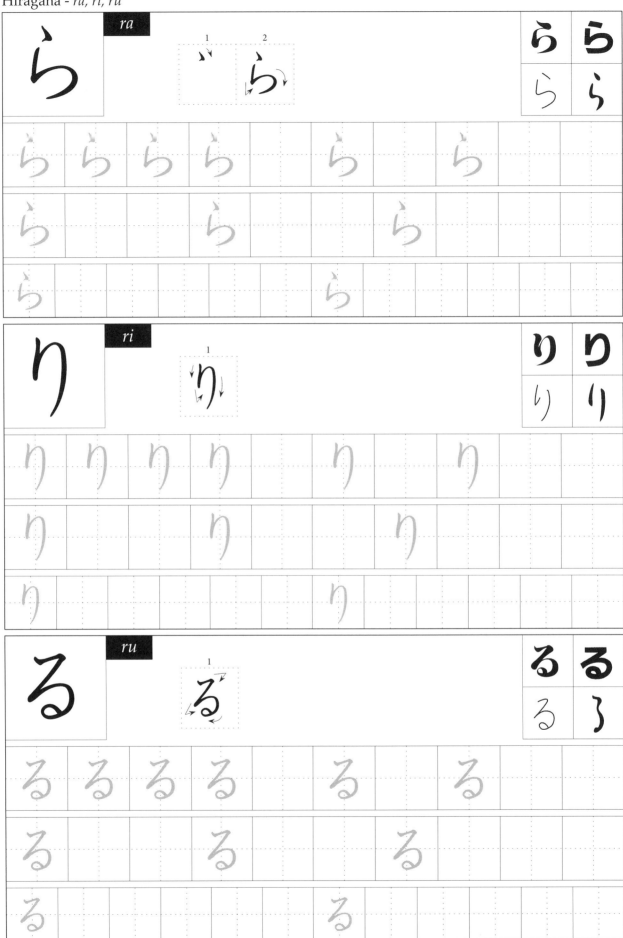

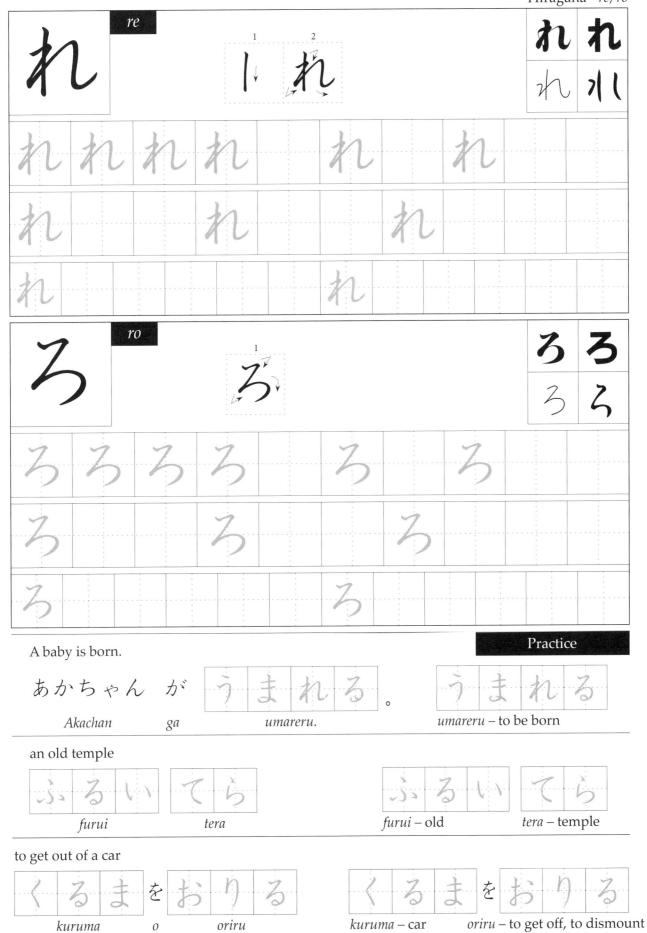

re

ro

A baby is born.

あかちゃん が うまれる 。　うまれる

Akachan　　*ga*　　*umareru.*　　*umareru* – to be born

an old temple

ふるい てら　　ふるい てら

furui　　*tera*　　*furui* – old　　*tera* – temple

to get out of a car

くるま を おりる　　くるま を おりる

kuruma　　*o*　　*oriru*　　*kuruma* – car　　*oriru* – to get off, to dismount

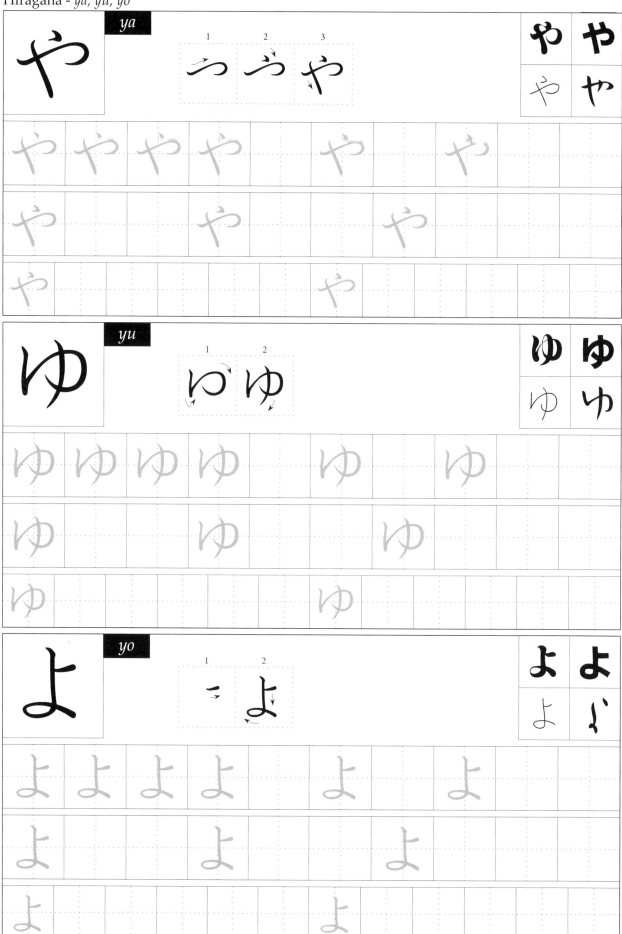

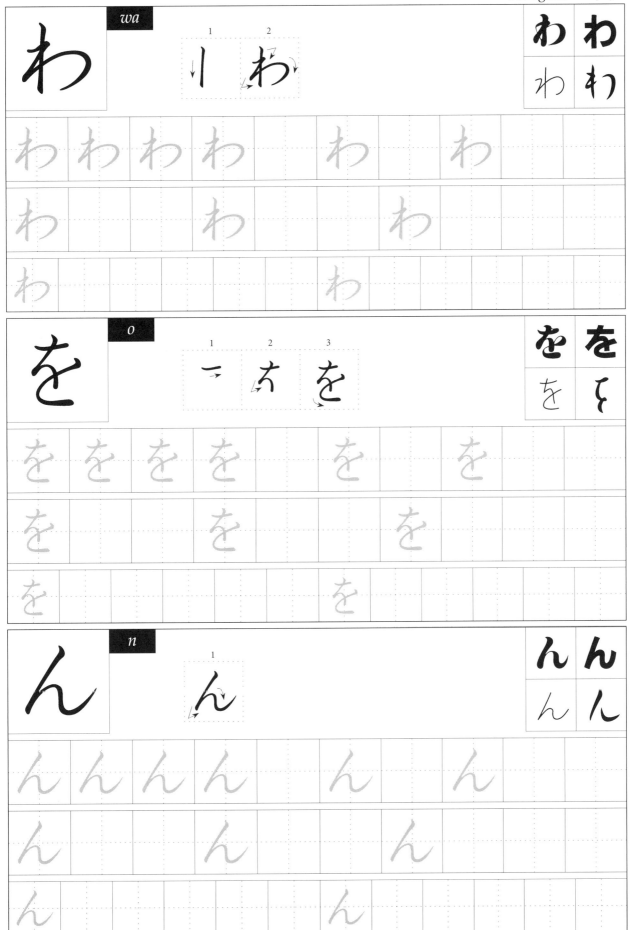

I read books every day.

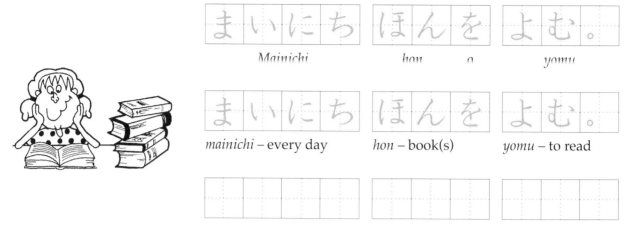

まいにち　ほんを　よむ。
Mainichi　hon　o　yomu

まいにち　ほんを　よむ。
mainichi – every day　　*hon* – book(s)　　*yomu* – to read

The ship sails slowly across the harbor.

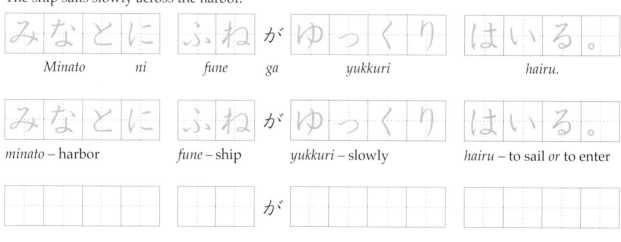

みなとに　ふねが　ゆっくり　はいる。
Minato　ni　fune　ga　yukkuri　hairu.

みなとに　ふねが　ゆっくり　はいる。
minato – harbor　　*fune* – ship　　*yukkuri* – slowly　　*hairu* – to sail *or* to enter

が

The bear lives in the mountains.

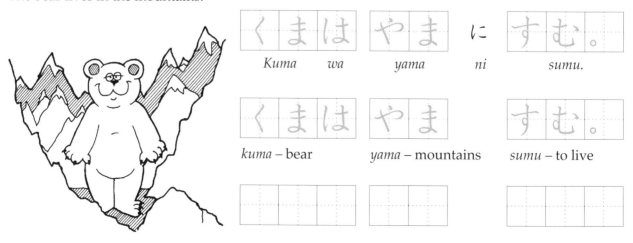

くまは　やま　に　すむ。
Kuma　wa　yama　ni　sumu.

くまは　やま　すむ。
kuma – bear　　*yama* – mountains　　*sumu* – to live

The river is below those mountains over there.

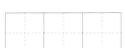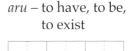

Kawa wa ano yama no susono ni aru.

kawa – river   *ano* – over there   *yama* – mountain   *susono* – foothills   *aru* – to have, to be, to exist

The famous Ms Yamaha

yūmei   na   Yamaha san

yūmei – famous   *Yamaha san* – Mr / Ms Yamaha

I will contact you tomorrow.

Ashita anata ni renraku shimasu.

ashita – tomorrow   *anata* – you   *renraku* – contact   *suru* – to do   *shimasu* – to do (formal)

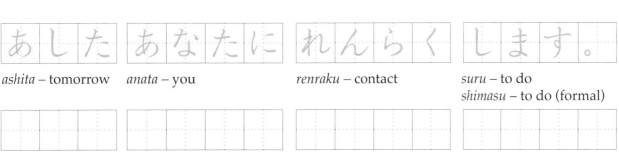

Pardon my rudeness.

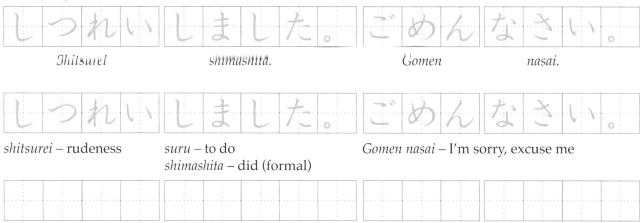

しつれいしました。 ごめんなさい。
Shitsurei *shimashita.* *Gomen* *nasai.*

しつれいしました。 ごめんなさい。

shitsurei – rudeness
suru – to do
shimashita – did (formal)

Gomen nasai – I'm sorry, excuse me

The bullet train is fast.

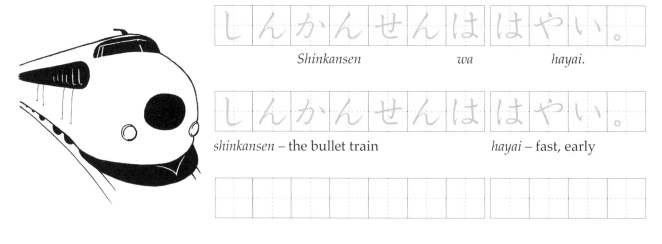

しんかんせんははやい。
Shinkansen *wa* *hayai.*

しんかんせんははやい。

shinkansen – the bullet train

hayai – fast, early

Everybody was really happy.

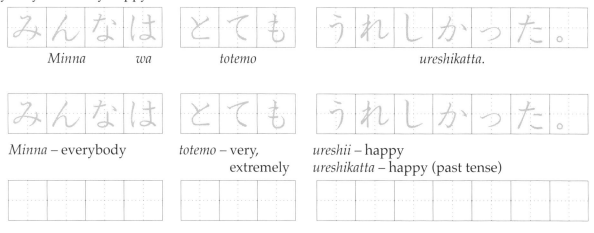

みんなは とても うれしかった。
Minna *wa* *totemo* *ureshikatta.*

みんなは とても うれしかった。

Minna – everybody

totemo – very, extremely

ureshii – happy
ureshikatta – happy (past tense)

I'll buy some vegetables at the vegetable store.

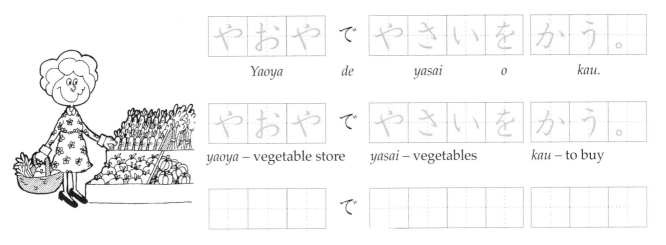

や　お　や　で　や　さ　い　を　か　う。

Yaoya　de　yasai　o　kau.

や　お　や　で　や　さ　い　を　か　う。

yaoya – vegetable store　　*yasai* – vegetables　　*kau* – to buy

で

That girl is very kind.

あ　の　お　ね　え　さ　ん　は　や　さ　し　い　です。

Ano　onē-san　wa　yasashii　desu.

あ　の　お　ね　え　さ　ん　は　や　さ　し　い　です。

ano – that　　*onē-san* – elder sister, girl　　*yasashii* – kind, gentle

です。

The cars have stopped.

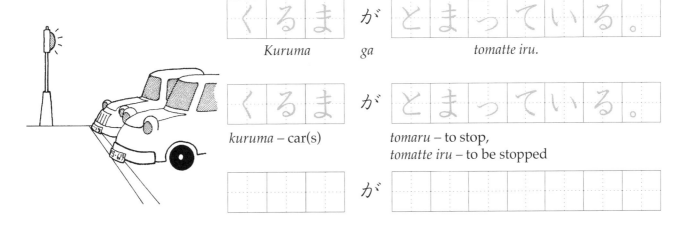

く　る　ま　が　と　ま　っ　て　い　る。

Kuruma　ga　tomatte iru.

く　る　ま　が　と　ま　っ　て　い　る。

kuruma – car(s)　　*tomaru* – to stop,
tomatte iru – to be stopped

が

Of the forty-six basic hiragana characters, some begin with a voiced consonant such as 'n' or 'm' while others begin with an unvoiced consonant.

The characters that begin with an unvoiced consonant are the *ka* series, the *sa* series, the *ta* series and the *ha* series of characters. These characters have voiced counterparts, as shown in the list below. The voiced characters are known as *dakuon*, meaning 'hardened sound.'

Dakuon are denoted by two small strokes at the top right-hand side of the character.

In addition to the *dakuon*, the characters *ha, hi, fu, he,* and *ho* have the semi-voiced counterparts, *pa, pi, pu, pe,* and *po*, denoted by a small circle at the top right-hand side of the character. The semi-voiced characters are known as *handakuon*, meaning 'half-hardened sound.'

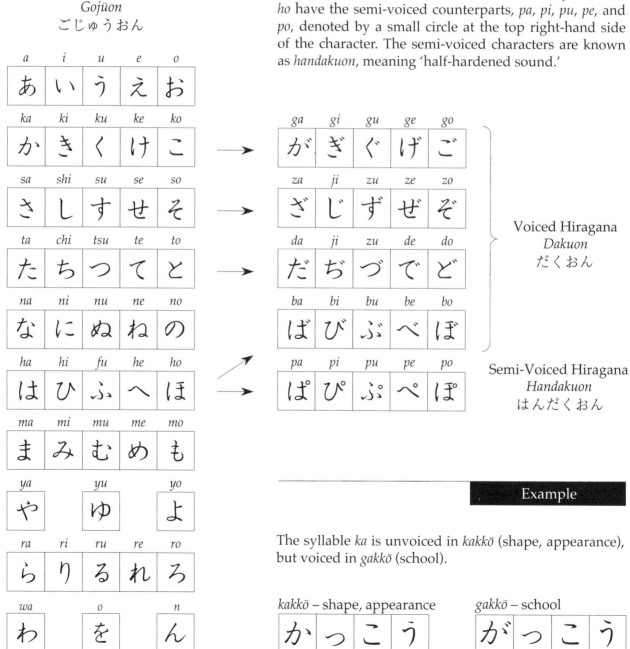

Basic Hiragana
Gojūon
ごじゅうおん

Voiced Hiragana
Dakuon
だくおん

Semi-Voiced Hiragana
Handakuon
はんだくおん

The syllable *ka* is unvoiced in *kakkō* (shape, appearance), but voiced in *gakkō* (school).

kakkō – shape, appearance

gakkō – school

In addition to the characters on the adjacent page, there is a set of contracted sounds.

The contracted sounds are formed by combining characters that have the 'i' sound (*ki*, *shi*, *chi*, *ni*, *hi*, *mi*, and *ri*) with *ya*, *yu*, or *yo*, as shown below. The resultant contraction is pronounced as a single syllable, and is written with the second character (*ya*, *yu* or *yo*) smaller than the preceding character.

The contracted sounds are called *yōon*, meaning 'shortened sound.' Like the basic hiragana, the contracted sounds have voiced and semi-voiced counterparts.

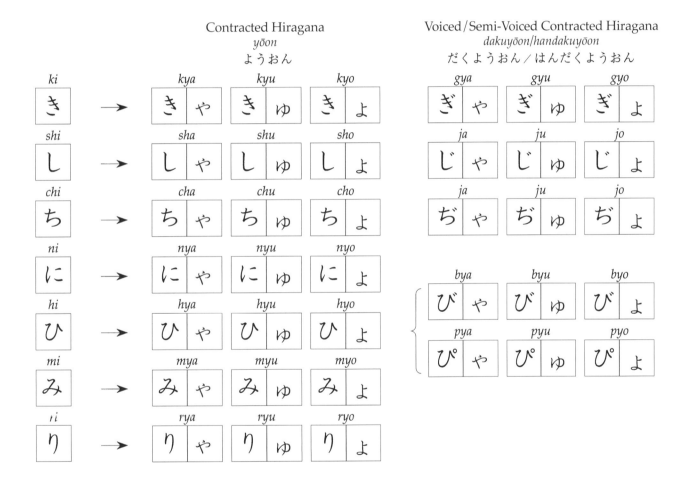

The syllables *bi* and *yo* as separate, uncontracted sounds in *biyōin* (beauty parlor), but as contracted sounds in *byōin* (hospital).

biyoin – beauty parlor

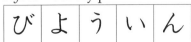

byōin – hospital

Can I have a receipt, please?

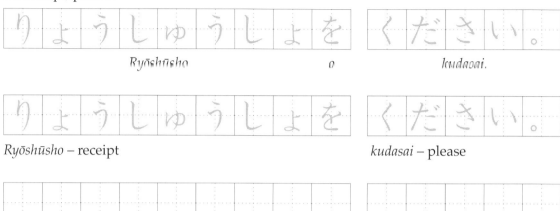

りょうしゅうしょを　　　　ください。
Ryōshūsho 　　　　　　　　*o* 　　　　*kudasai.*

りょうしゅうしょを　　　　ください。

Ryōshūsho – receipt 　　　　　　*kudasai* – please

Just a moment!

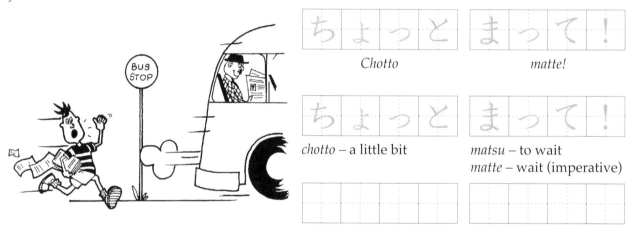

ちょっと　まって！
Chotto 　　　*matte!*

ちょっと　まって！

chotto – a little bit 　　　*matsu* – to wait
　　　　　　　　　　　　matte – wait (imperative)

I'll catch the train to Jiyugaoka.

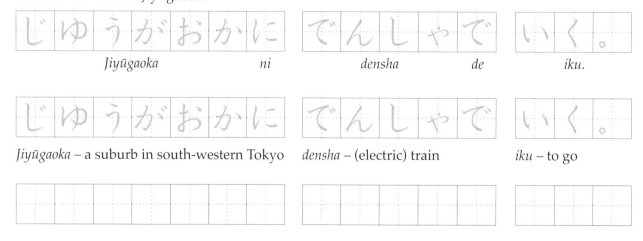

じゅうがおかに　でんしゃで　いく。
Jiyūgaoka 　　　*ni* 　　　*densha* 　*de* 　　*iku.*

じゅうがおかに　でんしゃで　いく。

Jiyūgaoka – a suburb in south-western Tokyo 　*densha* – (electric) train 　*iku* – to go

The food at Japanese inns is delicious.

りょかんの
Ryokan   *no*

りょうりは
ryōri   *wa*

おいしい。
oishii.

りょかんの

りょうりは

おいしい。

ryokan – Japanese style inn

ryōri – cooking

oishii – delicious

A classroom

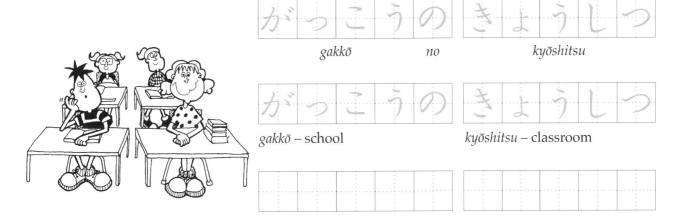

がっこうの
gakkō   *no*

きょうしつ
kyōshitsu

がっこうの

きょうしつ

gakkō – school

kyōshitsu – classroom

Dinner is not ready yet.

ばんごはんは
Ban gohan   *wa*

まだ
mada

できていない。
dekite inai.

ばんごはんは

まだ

できていない。

ban gohan – evening meal

mada – still, yet

dekiru – to be ready *or* to be possible
dekite inai – not ready

I had an injection today.

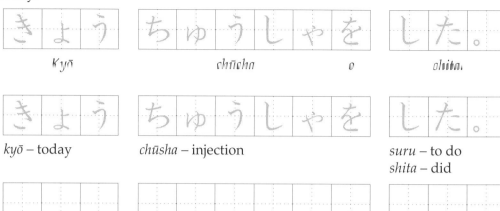

き	ょ	う

Kyō

ち	ゅ	う	し	ゃ	を

chūsha　　　　　*o*

し	た	。

shita.

き	ょ	う

kyō – today

ち	ゅ	う	し	ゃ	を

chūsha – injection

し	た	。

suru – to do
shita – did

The goldfish swim.

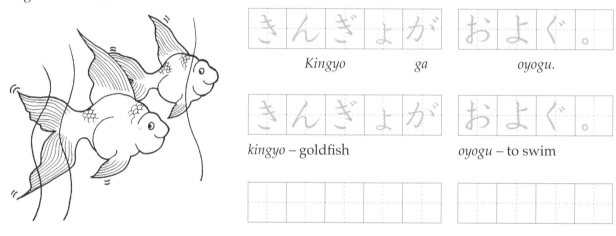

き	ん	ぎ	ょ	が

Kingyo　　　*ga*

お	よ	ぐ	。

oyogu.

き	ん	ぎ	ょ	が

kingyo – goldfish

お	よ	ぐ	。

oyogu – to swim

Ryota has become ill.

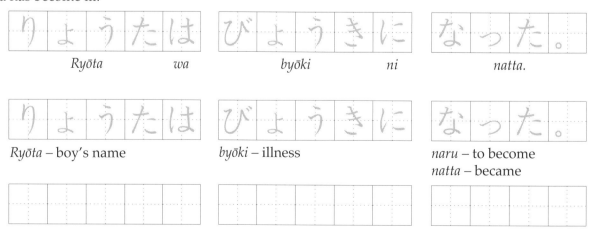

り	ょ	う	た	は

Ryōta　　　*wa*

び	ょ	う	き	に

byōki　　　*ni*

な	っ	た	。

natta.

り	ょ	う	た	は

Ryōta – boy's name

び	ょ	う	き	に

byōki – illness

な	っ	た	。

naru – to become
natta – became

Don't worry, it's okay.

たいじょうぶ、しんぱい しないで。

Daijōbu *shinpai* *shinai* *de.*

たいじょうぶ、しんぱい しないで。

daijōbu – alright, safe

shinpai – worry, concern

suru – to do
shinai de – don't do

A train ticket

でんしゃの きっぷ

densha *no* *kippu*

でんしゃの きっぷ

densha – (electric) train

kippu – ticket

That bicycle over there is in the way.

あそこの じてんしゃが じゃまだ。

Asoko *no* *jitensha* *ga* *jama* *da.*

あそこの じてんしゃが じゃまだ。

asoko – over there

jitensha – bicycle

jama – obstacle, hindrance
desu/da – is/is (informal)

The dumplings taste just right.

| ぎ | ょ | う | ざ | の | | あ | じ | が | | ち | ょ | う | ど | | い | い | 。 |

Gyōza　　　　　no　　　　　aji　ga　　　　chōdo　　　　　ii,

| ぎ | ょ | う | ざ | の | | あ | じ | が | | ち | ょ | う | ど | | い | い | 。 |

gyōza – Chinese dumplings　　*aji* – flavor　　*chōdo* – exactly　　*ii* – good

---

I drank the milk.

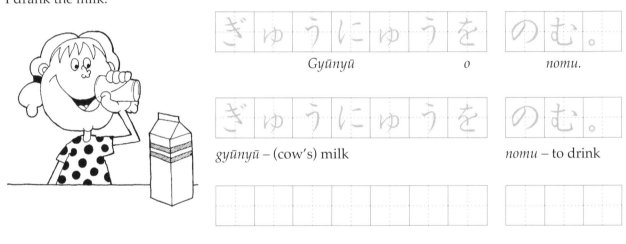

| ぎ | ゅ | う | に | ゅ | う | を | | の | む | 。 |

Gyūnyū　　　　　　　　o　　　　nomu.

| ぎ | ゅ | う | に | ゅ | う | を | | の | む | 。 |

gyūnyū – (cow's) milk　　　　*nomu* – to drink

I enjoy baseball practice.

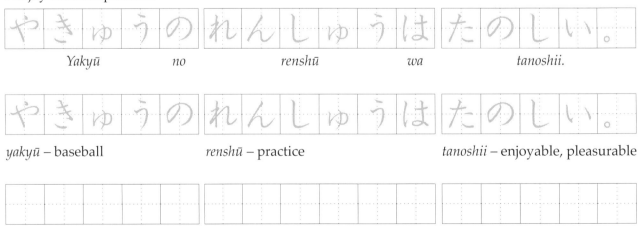

| や | き | ゅ | う | の | れ | ん | し | ゅ | う | は | た | の | し | い | 。 |

Yakyū　　　　no　　　renshū　　　　wa　　　tanoshii.

| や | き | ゅ | う | の | れ | ん | し | ゅ | う | は | た | の | し | い | 。 |

yakyū – baseball　　　　*renshū* – practice　　　　*tanoshii* – enjoyable, pleasurable

Wait your turn properly.

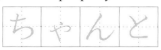

Chanto   *junban*   *o*   *matte.*

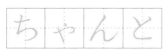

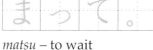

chanto – properly   *junban* – turn, order   *matsu* – to wait
matte – wait (imperative)

Eight hundred and nineteen

$$\begin{aligned}800 + \\ 10 \\ 9 \\ \hline 819\end{aligned}$$

happyaku   *jūkyū*

happyaku – eight hundred   *jūkyū* – nineteen

The address of the junior high school

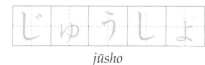

chūgakkō   *no*   *jūsho*

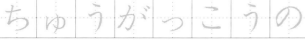

chūgakkō – junior high school   *jūsho* – address

47

にほんかい
Japan Sea

ほっかいどう

さっぽろ

ほんしゅう

きょうと
かなざわ　ながの　せんだい
おおさか
にっこう
ひろしま　こうべ　とうきょう
ふくおか　なごや　よこはま
ながさき　なら
こうち
きゅうしゅう　しこく

たいへいよう
Pacific Ocean

おきなわ

なは

Japan consists of eight regions, five of which are on the main island, Honshū. They are:

とうほく　　(Tōhoku) North-eastern region
かんとう　　(Kantō) Area around Tōkyō and Yokohama
ちゅうぶ　　(Chūbu) Area west of Kantō, taking in Nagoya
きんき　　　(Kinki) Area around Ōsaka, Kyōto, Nara and Kōbe
ちゅうごく (Chūgoku) Western end of Honshu, taking in Hiroshima

The three other major islands — Kyushū (which takes in Okinawa), Hokkaidō and Shikoku — are the other three regions.

Tōkyō

とうきょう

Ōsaka

おおさか

Yokohama

よこはま

Kyōto

きょうと

Hiroshima

ひろしま

Nagasaki

ながさき

Nikkō

にっこう

Fukuoka

ふくおか

Kanazawa

かなざわ

Sendai

せんだい

Nagoya

なごや

Kōbe

こうべ

Nagano

ながの

Nara

なら

Hokkaidō

ほっかいどう

Honshū

ほんしゅう

Shikoku

しこく

Kyūshū

きゅうしゅう

The clock goes tick tock tick tock.

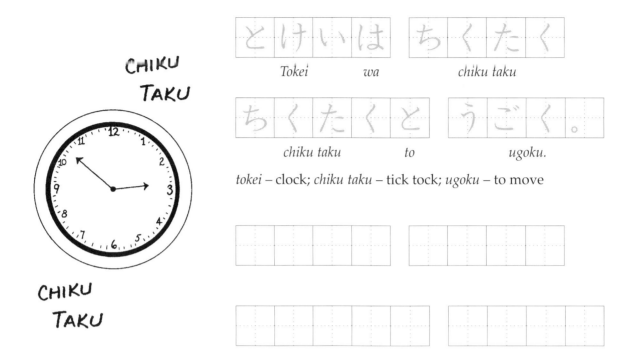

とけいは　ちくたく
Tokei　*wa*　*chiku taku*

ちくたくと　うごく。
chiku taku　*to*　*ugoku.*

tokei – clock; *chiku taku* – tick tock; *ugoku* – to move

My elder sister angrily stomped along the corridor.

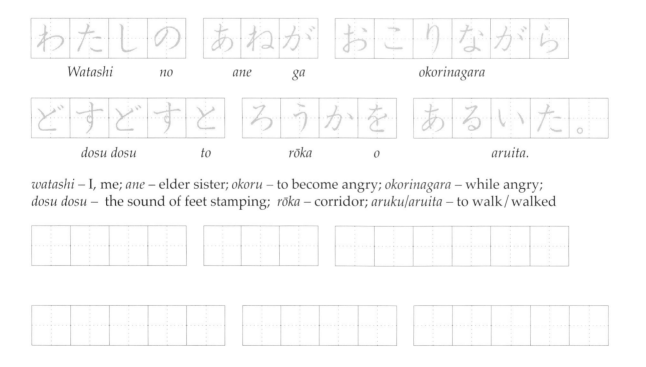

わたしの　あねが　おこりながら
Watashi　*no*　*ane*　*ga*　*okorinagara*

どすどすと　ろうかを　あるいた。
dosu dosu　*to*　*rōka*　*o*　*aruita.*

watashi – I, me; *ane* – elder sister; *okoru* – to become angry; *okorinagara* – while angry;
dosu dosu – the sound of feet stamping; *rōka* – corridor; *aruku/aruita* – to walk/walked

I scrubbed the bathtub until it gleamed.

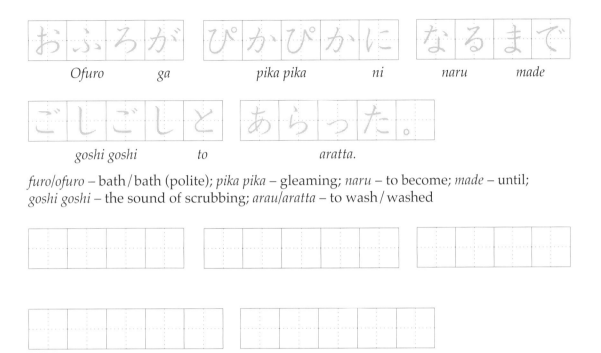

Ofuro — *ga* — *pika pika* — *ni* — *naru* — *made*

goshi goshi — *to* — *aratta.*

furo/ofuro – bath/bath (polite); *pika pika* – gleaming; *naru* – to become; *made* – until;
goshi goshi – the sound of scrubbing; *arau/aratta* – to wash/washed

The cat goes meow.

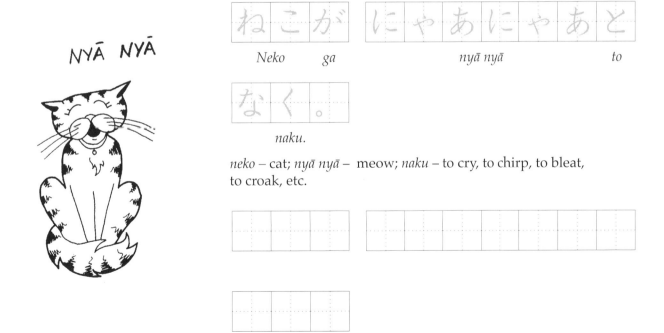

NYĀ NYĀ

Neko — *ga* — *nyā nyā* — *to*

naku.

neko – cat; *nyā nyā* – meow; *naku* – to cry, to chirp, to bleat,
to croak, etc.

I drink the water, gulp, gulp, gulp.

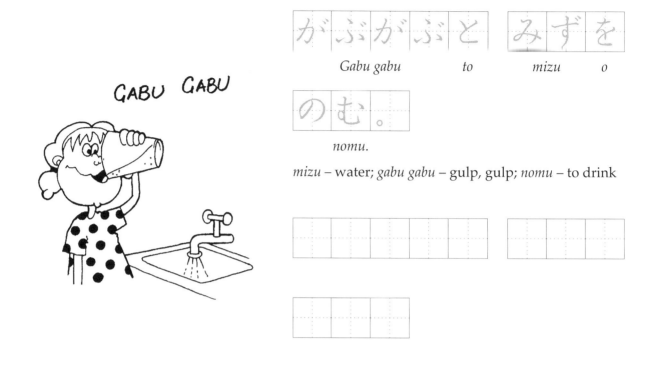

GABU GABU

がぶがぶと　みずを

Gabu gabu　　　　*to*　　　*mizu*　　*o*

のむ。

nomu.

mizu – water; *gabu gabu* – gulp, gulp; *nomu* – to drink

The students smiled excitedly as they left the classroom.

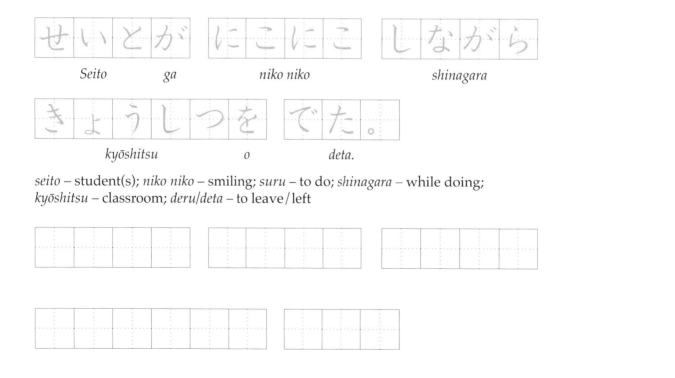

せいとが　にこにこ　しながら

Seito　　　*ga*　　　*niko niko*　　　　*shinagara*

きょうしつを　でた。

kyōshitsu　　　*o*　　　*deta.*

seito – student(s); *niko niko* – smiling; *suru* – to do; *shinagara* – while doing;
kyōshitsu – classroom; *deru/deta* – to leave/left

The rooster on the farm crows early in the morning.

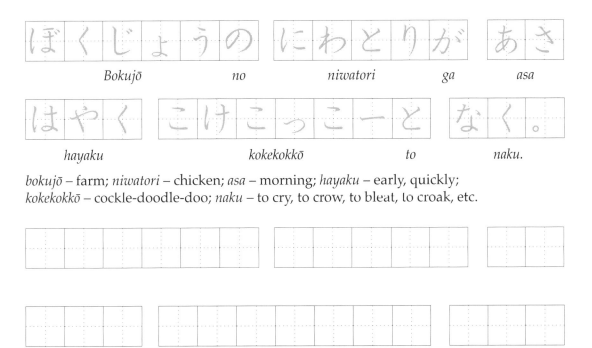

ぼ く じ ょ う の　に わ と り が　あ さ

Bokujō   *no*   *niwatori*   *ga*   *asa*

は や く　こ け こ っ こ ー と　な く 。

hayaku   *kokekokkō*   *to*   *naku.*

bokujō – farm; *niwatori* – chicken; *asa* – morning; *hayaku* – early, quickly;
kokekokkō – cockle-doodle-doo; *naku* – to cry, to crow, to bleat, lo croak, etc.

The frog croaks.

KERO KERO

か え る が　け ろ け ろ と

Kaeru   *ga*   *kero kero*   *to*

な く 。

naku.

kaeru – frog; *kero kero to naku* – to croak

The school student cracked his knuckles all through the lesson.

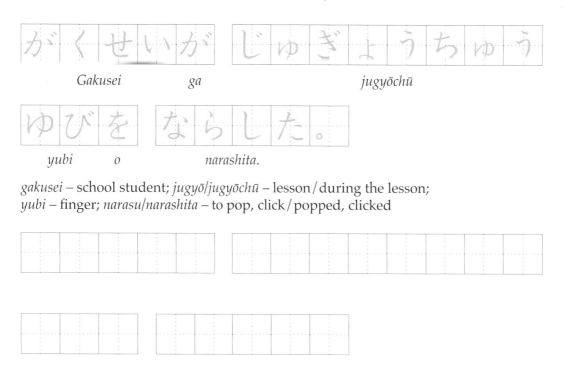

がくせいが　じゅぎょうちゅう

Gakusei　*ga*　*jugyōchū*

ゆびを　ならした。

yubi　*o*　*narashita.*

gakusei – school student; *jugyō/jugyōchū* – lesson / during the lesson;
yubi – finger; *narasu/narashita* – to pop, click / popped, clicked

---

I eat the rice, gobble, gobble, gobble.

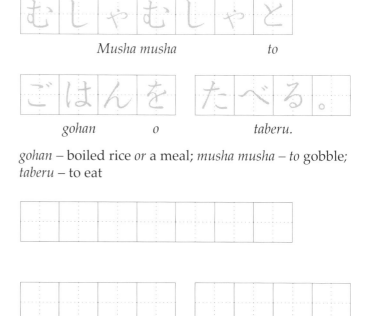

むしゃむしゃと

Musha musha　*to*

ごはんを　たべる。

gohan　*o*　*taberu.*

gohan – boiled rice *or* a meal; *musha musha* – *to* gobble;
taberu – to eat

The cow in the field goes moo.

Ushi   ga   nohara   de

mō mō   to   naku.

ushi – cow / bull; *nohara* – field, meadow;
mō mō – moo; *naku* – to cry, to bleat, to croak, etc.

The big beach ball is rolling across the sand.

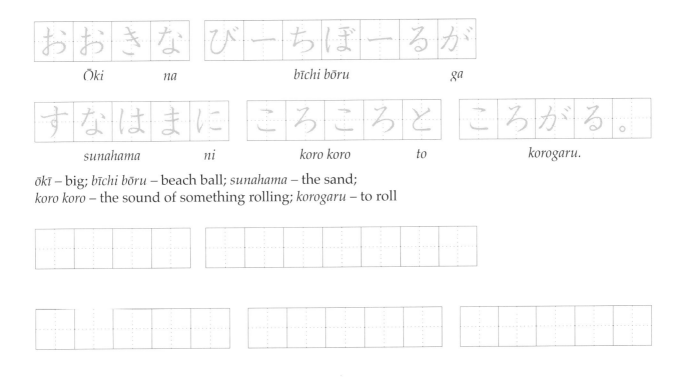

Ōki   na   bīchi bōru   ga

sunahama   ni   koro koro   to   korogaru.

ōkī – big; *bīchi bōru* – beach ball; *sunahama* – the sand;
koro koro – the sound of something rolling; *korogaru* – to roll

The baseball player hit the ball a long way with his bat.

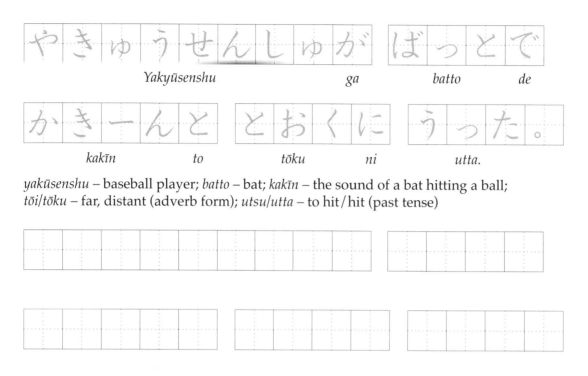

やきゅうせんしゅが ばっとで
Yakyūsenshu   *ga*   *batto*   *de*

かきーんと とおくに うった。
kakīn   *to*   *tōku*   *ni*   *utta.*

yakūsenshu – baseball player; *batto* – bat; *kakīn* – the sound of a bat hitting a ball; *tōi/tōku* – far, distant (adverb form); *utsu/utta* – to hit / hit (past tense)

I've caught a cold, atishoo!

HAKKUSHON !

かぜを ひいている、
Kaze   *o*   *hiite iru*

はっくしょん！
hakkushon!

kaze o hiku – to catch a cold; *kaze o hiite iru* – to have caught a cold; *hakkushon* – atishoo, ahchoo

The mouse squeaks in his hole.

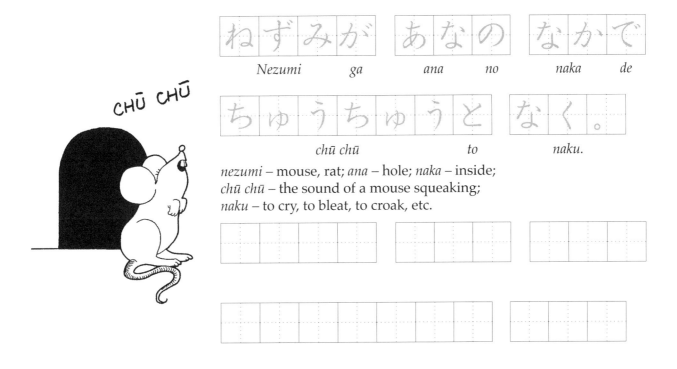

ねずみが　あなの　なかで

Nezumi　ga　ana　no　naka　de

ちゅうちゅうと　なく。

chū chū　to　naku.

nezumi – mouse, rat; *ana* – hole; *naka* – inside;
chū chū – the sound of a mouse squeaking;
naku – to cry, to bleat, to croak, etc.

The horse neighed, then clip-clopped away.

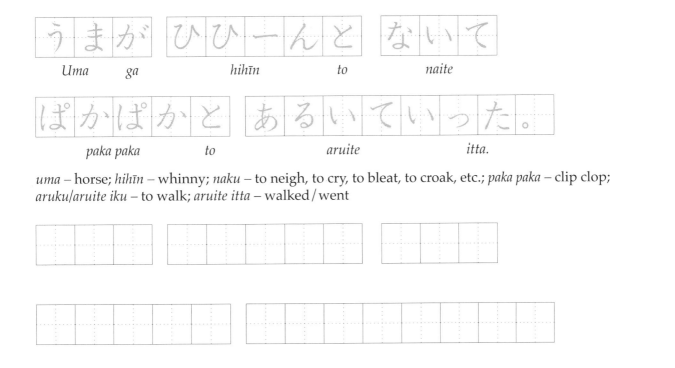

うまが　ひひーんと　ないて

Uma　ga　hihīn　to　naite

ぱかぱかと　あるいていった。

paka paka　to　aruite　itta.

uma – horse; *hihīn* – whinny; *naku* – to neigh, to cry, to bleat, to croak, etc.; *paka paka* – clip clop;
aruku/aruite iku – to walk; *aruite itta* – walked/went

kyōshitsu – classroom

きょうしつ

sensei – teacher

せんせい

seito – pupil

せいと

tsukue – desk

つくえ

tokei – clock

とけい

きょうしつ

え

こくばん

はな

よいこ

せいと

つくえ

いす

らんどせる

おとこのこ

ものさ

otoko no ko – boy

おとこのこ

onna no ko – girl

おんなのこ

randoseru – knapsack, schoolbag

らんどせる

e – picture

え

hon – book

ほ ん

isu – chair

い す

hana – flower

は な

bōshi – cap

ぼ う し

megane – glasses

め が ね

enpitsu – pencil

え ん ぴ つ

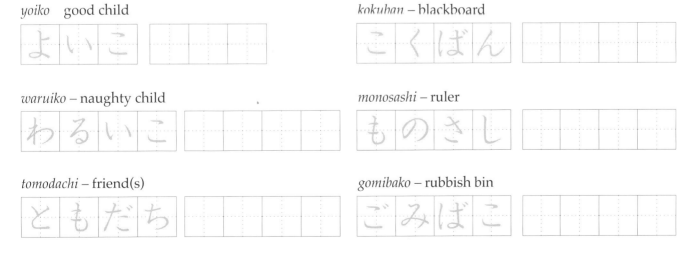

yoiko good child

よ い こ

kokuban – blackboard

こ く ば ん

waruiko – naughty child

わ る い こ

monosashi – ruler

も の さ し

tomodachi – friend(s)

と も だ ち

gomibako – rubbish bin

ご み ば こ

kazoku – family

かぞく

otōsan – father

おとうさん

okāsan – mother

おかあさん

kodomo – child, children

こども

okyakusan – guest, visitor *or* customer

おきゃくさん

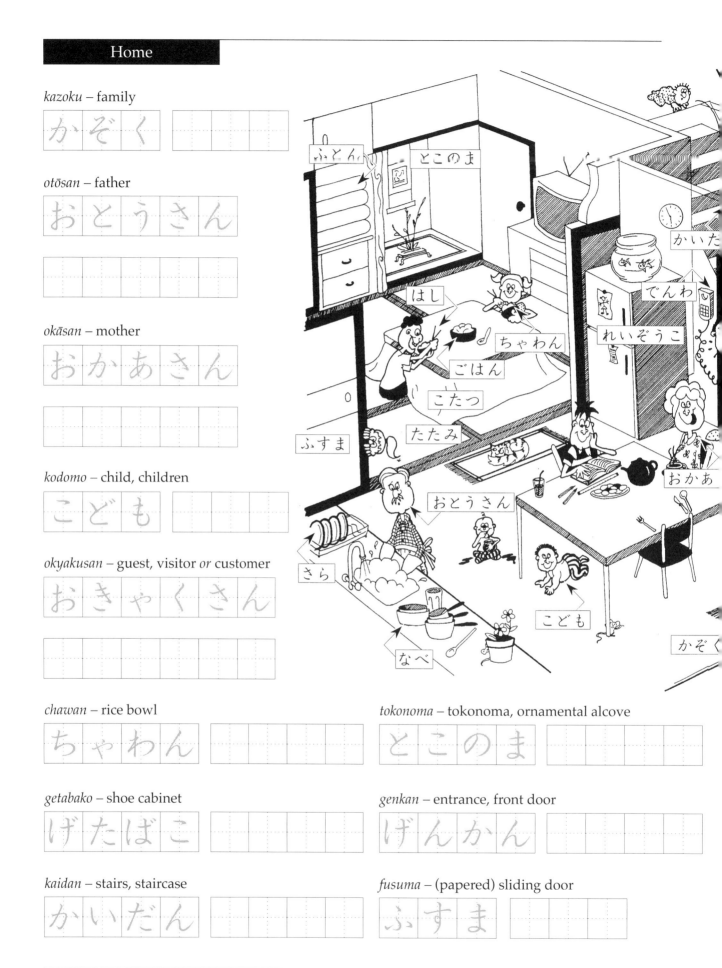

chawan – rice bowl

ちゃわん

tokonoma – tokonoma, ornamental alcove

とこのま

getabako – shoe cabinet

げたばこ

genkan – entrance, front door

げんかん

kaidan – stairs, staircase

かいだん

fusuma – (papered) sliding door

ふすま

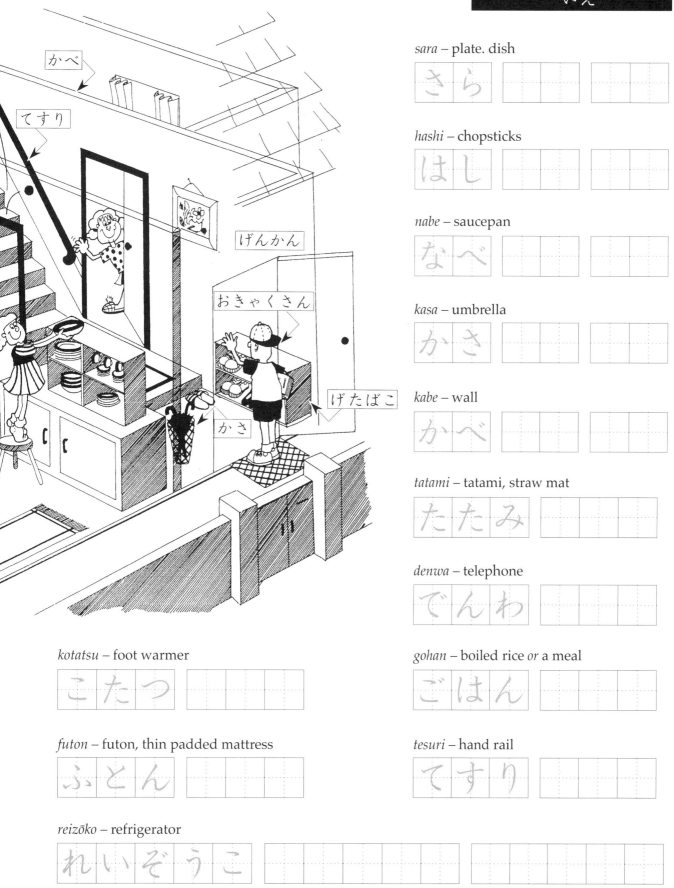

かべ

てすり

げんかん

おきゃくさん

かさ

げたばこ

sara – plate. dish

さ ら

hashi – chopsticks

は し

nabe – saucepan

な べ

kasa – umbrella

か さ

kabe – wall

か べ

tatami – tatami, straw mat

た た み

denwa – telephone

で ん わ

kotatsu – foot warmer

こ た つ

futon – futon, thin padded mattress

ふ と ん

reizōko – refrigerator

れ い ぞ う こ

gohan – boiled rice *or* a meal

ご は ん

tesuri – hand rail

て す り

Pen Pals

Haruka Watanabe is taking her summer vacation in a popular resort near Tokyo. She has written the following letter to her friend, Akira Hashimoto. Copy the letter into the space provided.

　あきらくん　おげんきですか。
わたしは　げんきです。　なつ
やすみは　たのしいですか。
わたしは　いずに　きています。
まいにち　およいでいます。
うみは　とても　きれいです。
さようなら。
8がつ11にち　　　　はるかより

Vocabulary

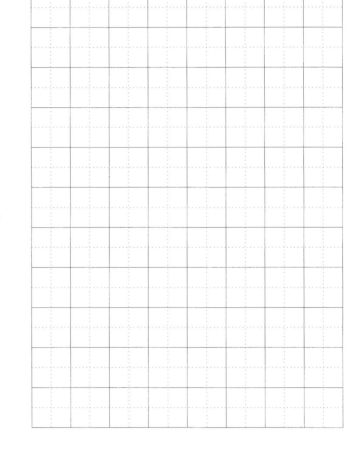

kun – boy's honorific suffix
ogenki – vigor, vitality (polite)
watashi – I
genki – vigor, vitality
natsu – summer
yasumi – holiday, vacation
tanoshii – fun, pleasurable
kuru – to come
kite iru/kite imasu – to have come
mainichi – every day
oyogu – to swim
oyoide iru/imasu – to be swimming
umi – the ocean
totemo – very, extremely
kirei – pretty, clean
sayōnara – farewell
gatsu – month
nichi – day
chan – girl's honorific suffix
tegami – letter
otegami – letter (polite)
arigatō – thank you
boku – I (used by young males)
~mo – ~ too
hanabi – fireworks
taikai – festival
ashita – tomorrow
iku/ikimasu – to go
suki – to like

The letter below is Akira Hashimoto's reply. Copy the letter into the space provided.

はるかちゃん　おてがみ　あ
りがとう。ぼくは　げんきで
す。　ぼくのなつやすみも
たのしいです。　ぼくは　あし
た　はなび　たいかいに　いき
ます。　ぼくは　はなびが　と
ても　すきです。　さようなら。
8がつ14か　あきらより

Exercises

1. Translate the letters, then answer the following questions.
2. Where is Haruka taking her summer vacation? ______
3. How is she spending her time? ______
4. What is Akira doing on his vacation? ______
5. On what dates were the letters written? ______

The Beach

I swim between the flags.

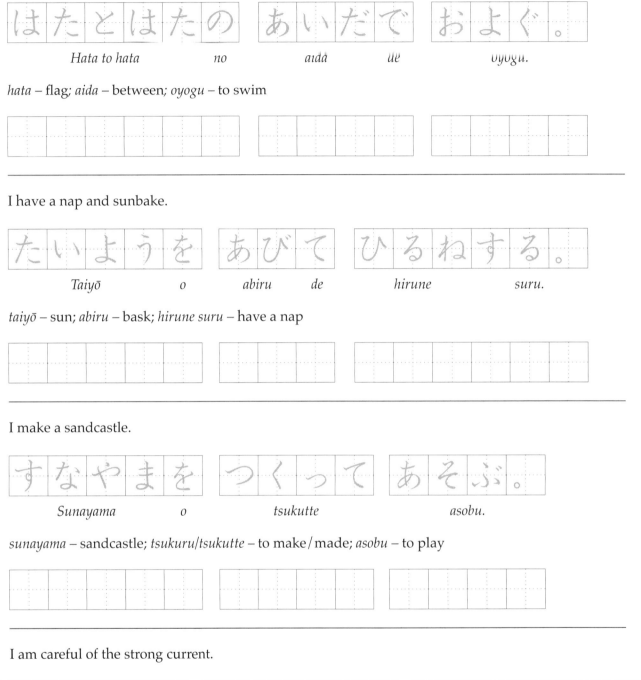

はたとはたの　あいだで　およぐ。

Hata to hata　no　aida　de　oyogu.

hata – flag; *aida* – between; *oyogu* – to swim

I have a nap and sunbake.

たいようを　あびて　ひるねする。

Taiyō　o　abiru　de　hirune　suru.

taiyō – sun; *abiru* – bask; *hirune suru* – have a nap

I make a sandcastle.

すなやまを　つくって　あそぶ。

Sunayama　o　tsukutte　asobu.

sunayama – sandcastle; *tsukuru/tsukutte* – to make/made; *asobu* – to play

I am careful of the strong current.

ひきしおが　つよいから　きをつける。

Hikishio　ga　tsuyoi　kara　ki　o　tsukeru.

hikishio – current during low tide; *tsuyoi* – strong; *ki o tsukeru* – to be careful

The water is too cold for swimming.

みずが　つめたくて　はいれない。

Mizu　*ga*　*tsumetaku*　*te*　*hairenai.*

mizu – water; *tsumetai* – cold; *hairu* – to go in; *hairenai* – can't go in

I am almost dumped by the waves.

なみに　ながされそうに　なる。

Nami　*ni*　*nagasaresō*　*ni*　*naru.*

nami – wave; *nagasaresō ni* – almost washed away, almost dumped; *naru* – to be

The seagulls steal the food.

かもめは　たべものを　ぬすむ。

Kamome　*wa*　*tabemono*　*o*　*nusumu.*

kamome – seagull; *tabemono* – food; *nusumu* – to steal

I stroll by the beach and gaze at the sunset.

はまを　さんぽして　ゆうひをみる。

Hama　*o*　*sanpo*　*shite*　*yūhi*　*o*　*miru.*

hama – beach; *sanpo* – stroll; *yūhi* – sunset; *miru* – to see

I apply the sunscreen.

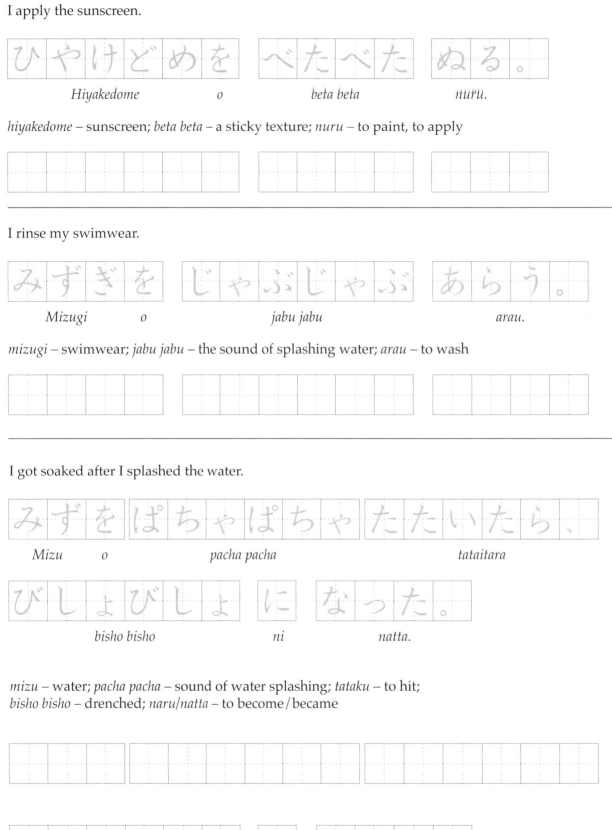

ひ や け ど め を　べ た べ た　ぬ る 。

Hiyakedome　　*o*　　*beta beta*　　*nuru.*

hiyakedome – sunscreen; *beta beta* – a sticky texture; *nuru* – to paint, to apply

I rinse my swimwear.

み ず ぎ を　じ ゃ ぶ じ ゃ ぶ　あ ら う 。

Mizugi　　*o*　　*jabu jabu*　　*arau.*

mizugi – swimwear; *jabu jabu* – the sound of splashing water; *arau* – to wash

I got soaked after I splashed the water.

み ず を ぱ ち ゃ ぱ ち ゃ た た い た ら 、

Mizu　　*o*　　*pacha pacha*　　*tataitara*

び し ょ び し ょ　に　な っ た 。

bisho bisho　　*ni*　　*natta.*

mizu – water; *pacha pacha* – sound of water splashing; *tataku* – to hit;
bisho bisho – drenched; *naru/natta* – to become/became

The sun is very warm, so it is likely my skin will burn.

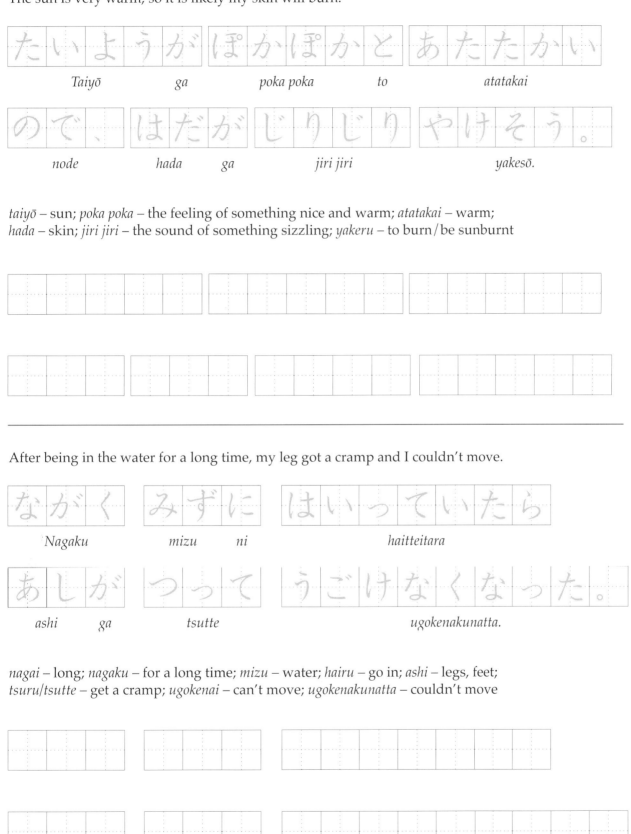

たいようが　ぽかぽかと　あたたかい

Taiyō　ga　poka poka　to　atatakai

ので、　はだが　じりじり　やけそう。

node　hada　ga　jiri jiri　yakesō.

taiyō – sun; *poka poka* – the feeling of something nice and warm; *atatakai* – warm;
hada – skin; *jiri jiri* – the sound of something sizzling; *yakeru* – to burn / be sunburnt

After being in the water for a long time, my leg got a cramp and I couldn't move.

ながく　みずに　はいっていたら

Nagaku　mizu　ni　haitteitara

あしが　つって　うごけなくなった。

ashi　ga　tsutte　ugokenakunatta.

nagai – long; *nagaku* – for a long time; *mizu* – water; *hairu* – go in; *ashi* – legs, feet;
tsuru/tsutte – get a cramp; *ugokenai* – can't move; *ugokenakunatta* – couldn't move

The Shopping Center

Clothes are now on sale and cheap.

いまは　やすうりで　ふくがやすい。

Ima　wa　yasūri　de　fuku　ga　yasui.

ima – now; *yasūri* – sale; *fuku* – clothes; *yasui* – cheap

The shops are packed on the weekend.

しゅうまつは　みせが　こんでいる。

Shūmatsu　wa　mise　ga　kondeiru.

shūmatsu – weekend; *mise* – shops; *kondeiru* – crowded

The car park is full.

ちゅうしゃじょうは　まんしゃだ。

Chūshajō　wa　mansha da.

chūshajō – car park; *mansha* – full (the term is only used for parking areas)

I buy candy at the cinema.

えいがかんで　あめを　かう。

Eigakan　de　ame　o　kau.

eigakan – cinema; *ame* – candy; *kau* – to buy

I buy *kimono* at the department store.

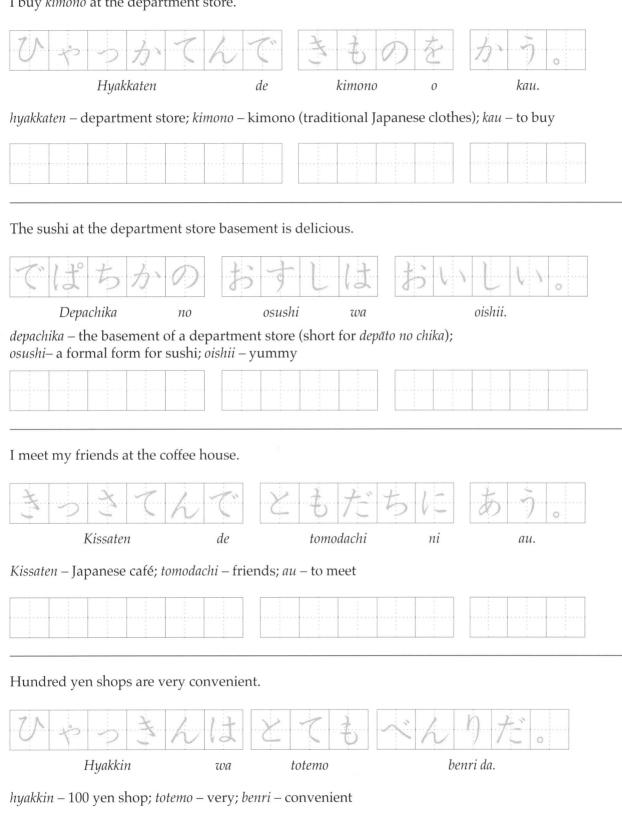

ひゃっかてんで きものを かう。

Hyakkaten　de　kimono　o　kau.

hyakkaten – department store; *kimono* – kimono (traditional Japanese clothes); *kau* – to buy

---

The sushi at the department store basement is delicious.

でぱちかの おすしは おいしい。

Depachika　no　osushi　wa　oishii.

depachika – the basement of a department store (short for *depāto no chika*);
osushi– a formal form for sushi; *oishii* – yummy

I meet my friends at the coffee house.

きっさてんで ともだちに あう。

Kissaten　de　tomodachi　ni　au.

Kissaten – Japanese café; *tomodachi* – friends; *au* – to meet

---

Hundred yen shops are very convenient.

ひゃっきんは とても べんりだ。

Hyakkin　wa　totemo　benri da.

hyakkin – 100 yen shop; *totemo* – very; *benri* – convenient

69

The shops are open until late today, because it's the weekend.

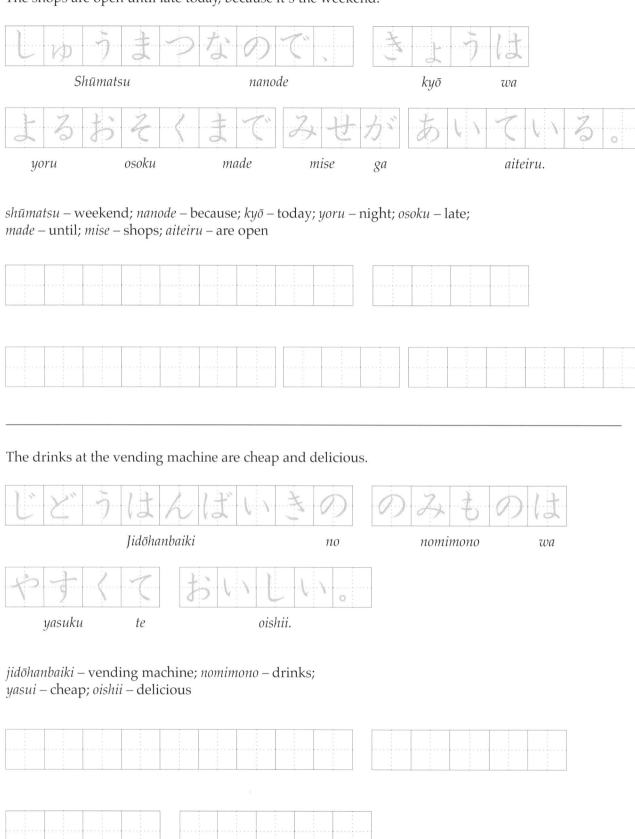

しゅうまつなので、 きょうは
Shūmatsu *nanode* *kyō* *wa*

よるおそくまで みせが あいている。
yoru *osoku* *made* *mise* *ga* *aiteiru.*

shūmatsu – weekend; *nanode* – because; *kyō* – today; *yoru* – night; *osoku* – late; *made* – until; *mise* – shops; *aiteiru* – are open

The drinks at the vending machine are cheap and delicious.

じどうはんばいきの のみものは
Jidōhanbaiki *no* *nomimono* *wa*

やすくて おいしい。
yasuku *te* *oishii.*

jidōhanbaiki – vending machine; *nomimono* – drinks; *yasui* – cheap; *oishii* – delicious

The Chinese restaurants are always noisy and full.

ちゅうかりょうりてんは　いつも

Chūkaryōriten *wa* *itsumo*

まんせきで、　がやがやと

manseki *de* *gaya gaya* *to*

そうぞうしい。

sōzōshii.

chūkaryōriten – Chinese restaurant; *itsumo* – always; *manseki* – when the seats are full *or* full;
gaya gaya – the noise of a large crowd chatting; *sōzōshii* – noisy

It's raining today, so I will study at the library.

あめが　しとしと　ふっている　から

Ame *ga* *shito shito* *futteiru* *kara*

としょかんで　べんきょうする。

toshokan *de* *benkyō* *suru.*

ame – rain; *shito shito* – the sound of light rain; *futteiru* – raining; *kara* – since/because;
toshokan – library; *benkyō suru* – to study

I go and see the cherry blossoms with my family.

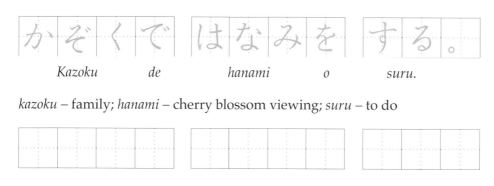

Kazoku   de   hanami   o   suru.

kazoku – family; *hanami* – cherry blossom viewing; *suru* – to do

---

We made homemade lunch together.

Obento   o   minna   de   tsukuru.

Obento – Japanese homemade lunch box; *minna* – everyone; *tsukuru* – to make

Fried rice balls are yummy.

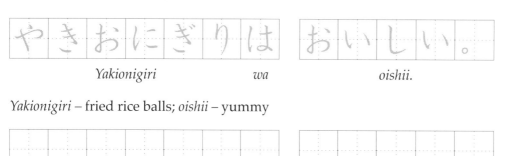

Yakionigiri   wa   oishii.

Yakionigiri – fried rice balls; *oishii* – yummy

There are a lot of insects.

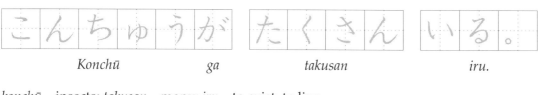

Konchū   ga   takusan   iru.

konchū – insects; *takusan* – many; *iru* – to exist, to live

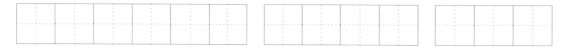

Fireflies fly at night in summer.

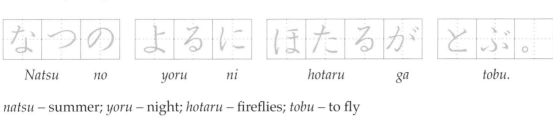

Natsu　　no　　yoru　　ni　　hotaru　　ga　　tobu.

natsu – summer; *yoru* – night; *hotaru* – fireflies; *tobu* – to fly

I catch bugs in the mountain.

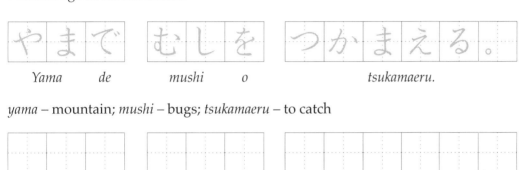

Yama　　de　　mushi　　o　　tsukamaeru.

yama – mountain; *mushi* – bugs; *tsukamaeru* – to catch

The sun is bright.

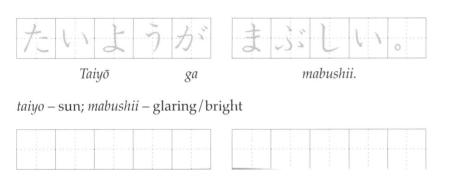

Taiyō　　ga　　mabushii.

taiyo – sun; *mabushii* – glaring/bright

The cicadas are noisy.

Semi　　no　　nakigoe　　ga　　urusai.

Semi – cicadas; *nakigoe* – the sound animals and insects make, sound; *urusai* – noisy

A lot of children are playing at the playground.

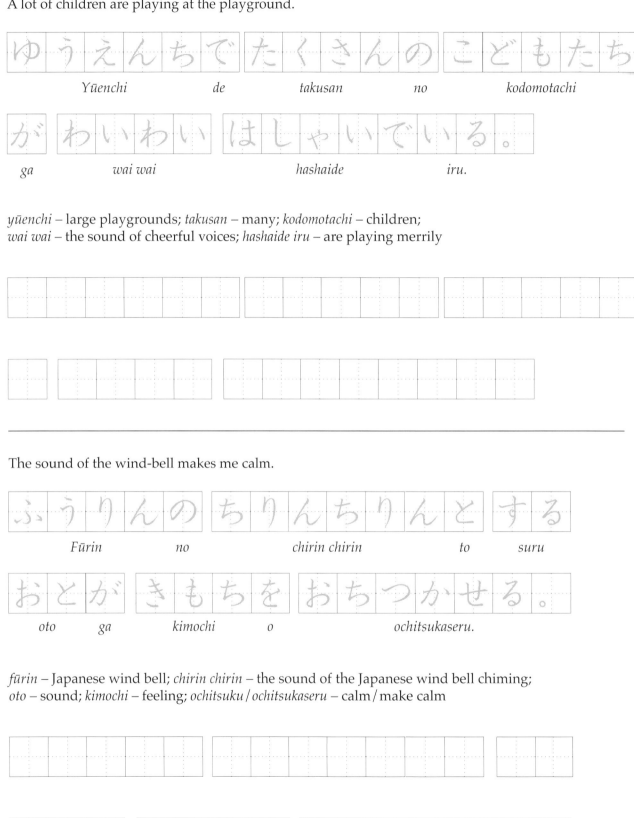

ゆうえんちで　たくさんの　こどもたち

Yūenchi　　*de*　　*takusan*　　*no*　　*kodomotachi*

が　わいわい　はしゃいでいる。

ga　*wai wai*　　*hashaide*　　*iru.*

yūenchi – large playgrounds; *takusan* – many; *kodomotachi* – children;
wai wai – the sound of cheerful voices; *hashaide iru* – are playing merrily

The sound of the wind-bell makes me calm.

ふうりんの　ちりんちりんと　する

Fūrin　　*no*　　*chirin chirin*　　*to*　*suru*

おとが　きもちを　おちつかせる。

oto　*ga*　*kimochi*　*o*　　*ochitsukaseru.*

fūrin – Japanese wind bell; *chirin chirin* – the sound of the Japanese wind bell chiming;
oto – sound; *kimochi* – feeling; *ochitsuku / ochitsukaseru* – calm / make calm

In summer, I wear a *yukata* and go to the festival with everyone.

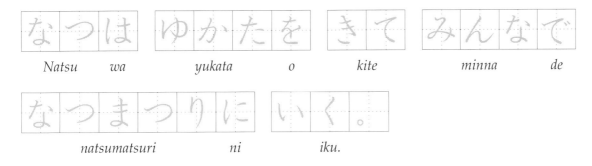

なつは　ゆかたを　きて　みんなで

Natsu *wa* *yukata* *o* *kite* *minna* *de*

なつまつりに　いく。

natsumatsuri *ni* *iku.*

natsu – summer; *yukata* – a casual cotton kimono; *kiru* – to wear; *minna* – everyone;
natsumatsuri – summer festival; *iku* – to go

The people in the village all gather and do the Obon festival dance.

むらの　ひとが　みな　あつまって

Mura *no* *hito* *ga* *mina* *atsumatte*

ぼんおどりを　する。

bon-odori *o* *suru.*

mura – village; *hito* – people; *mina* – everyone (same as *minna*); *atsumaru* – to gather;
bon-odori – the Obon festival dance; *suru* – to do

The teacher's explanation is boring.

せんせいの　はなしが　つまらない。

Sensei　*no*　*hanashi*　*ga*　*tsumaranai.*

Sensei – teacher; *hanashi* – story, speech; what the person is saying; *tsumaranai* – boring

I arrive late for class.

じゅぎょうに　ちこくする。

Jugyō　*ni*　*chikoku*　*suru.*

jugyō – class; *chikoku suru* – to arrive late

I join the judo club of the university.

だいがくの　じゅうどうぶに　はいる。

Daigaku　*no*　*judō-bu*　*ni*　*hairu.*

daigaku – university; *judō-bu* – judo club; *hairu* – to join, to enter

I have a lot of assignments at the end of the semester.

がっきまつは　かだいが　おおい。

Gakkimatsu　*wa*　*kadai*　*ga*　*ōi.*

gakkimatsu – end of semester; *kadai* – assignments; *ōi* – a lot of

I listen to a lecture on politics.

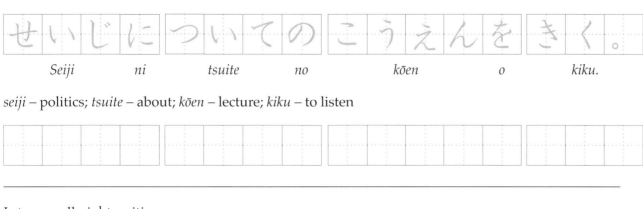

Seiji ni tsuite no kōen o kiku.

seiji – politics; *tsuite* – about; *kōen* – lecture; *kiku* – to listen

I stay up all night writing my essay.

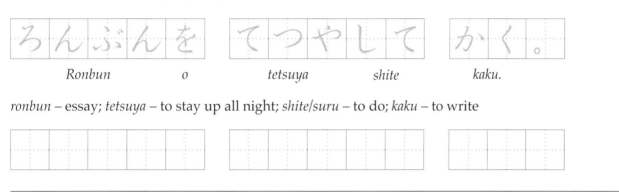

Ronbun o tetsuya shite kaku.

ronbun – essay; *tetsuya* – to stay up all night; *shite/suru* – to do; *kaku* – to write

Applying for graduate positions is very hard in Japan.

Nihon no shūkatsu wa taihen da.

Nihon – Japan; *shūkatsu* – college students looking for jobs (short for *shūshoku katsudō*); *taihen* – requires a lot of effort/hard

Go on to postgraduate studies.

Daigakuin ni susumu.

daigakuin – postgraduate; *susumu* – to move on to, to advance

You can graduate without attending class at my university.

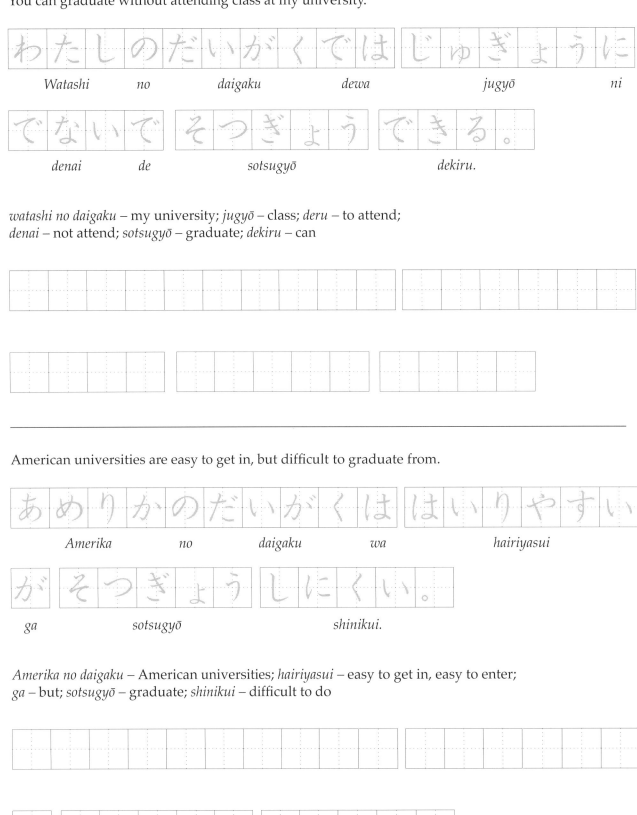

わたしのだいがくでは じゅぎょうに

Watashi no daigaku dewa jugyō ni

でないで そつぎょう できる。

denai de sotsugyō dekiru.

watashi no daigaku – my university; *jugyō* – class; *deru* – to attend;
denai – not attend; *sotsugyō* – graduate; *dekiru* – can

American universities are easy to get in, but difficult to graduate from.

あめりかのだいがくは はいりやすい

Amerika no daigaku wa hairiyasui

が そつぎょう しにくい。

ga sotsugyō shinikui.

Amerika no daigaku – American universities; *hairiyasui* – easy to get in, easy to enter;
ga – but; *sotsugyō* – graduate; *shinikui* – difficult to do

I make lots of friends and enjoy university life.

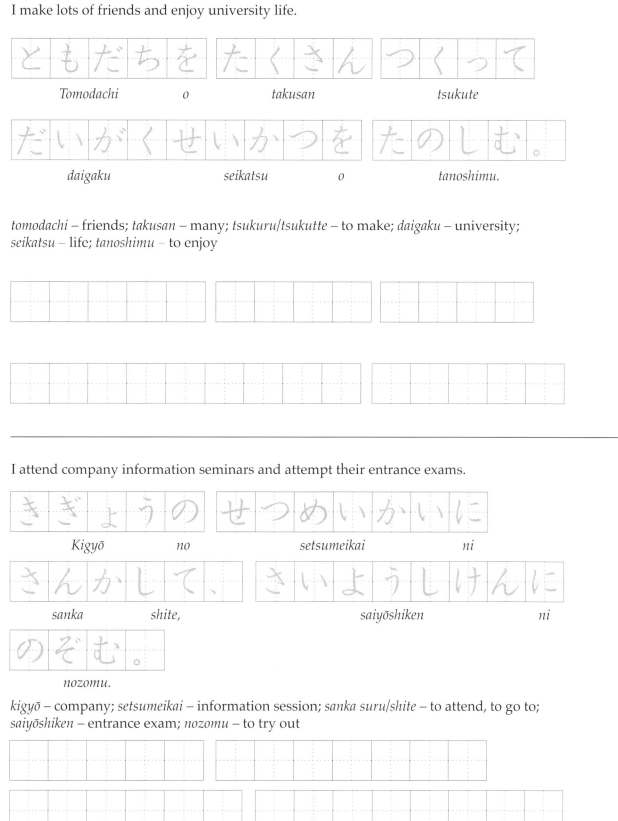

と　も　だ　ち　を　　た　く　さ　ん　　つ　く　っ　て

Tomodachi   *o*   *takusan*   *tsukute*

だ　い　が　く　せ　い　か　つ　を　　た　の　し　む。

daigaku   *seikatsu*   *o*   *tanoshimu.*

tomodachi – friends; *takusan* – many; *tsukuru/tsukutte* – to make; *daigaku* – university; *seikatsu* – life; *tanoshimu* – to enjoy

I attend company information seminars and attempt their entrance exams.

き　ぎ　ょ　う　の　　せ　つ　め　い　か　い　に

Kigyō   *no*   *setsumeikai*   *ni*

さ　ん　か　し　て、　　さ　い　よ　う　し　け　ん　に

sanka   *shite,*   *saiyōshiken*   *ni*

の　ぞ　む。

nozomu.

kigyō – company; *setsumeikai* – information session; *sanka suru/shite* – to attend, to go to; *saiyōshiken* – entrance exam; *nozomu* – to try out

A
abiru – bask
aida – between
aji – flavor
akai – red
aki – autumn
ana – hole
anata – you
ane – elder sister
ano – that, over there
arau – to wash
arigatō – thank you
aru – to have, to be, to exist
aruku – to walk
asa – morning
asatte – the day after tomorrow
ashi – leg, foot
ashita – tomorrow
asobu – to play
asoko – over there
asu – tomorrow
au – to meet

B
ban gohan – evening meal
batto – bat
bīchi bōru – beach ball
boku – I, me (used by males)
bokujō – farm
bōshi – cap
byōki – illness

C
chan – girl's honorific suffix
chanto – properly
chawan – rice bowl
chiisai – small
chōdo – exactly
chotto – a little bit
chūgakkō – junior high school
chūsha – injection

D
daigaku – university
daijōbu – alright, safe
de – by means of
dekiru – to be ready, to be possible
densha – (electric) train
denwa – telephone
desu – is, are
desu ne – isn't he, aren't they, etc.

E
e – picture
e – to, toward, for
eki – station
enpitsu – pencil

F
fune – ship
fuku – clothes
furo – bath
furui – old
fusuma – (papered) sliding door
futoi – large in diameter, thick, deep
futon – futon, thin padded mattress

G
gakkō – school
gakusei – school student
gatsu – month
genkan – entrance, front door
genki – vigor, vitality
getabako – shoe cabinet
gohan – boiled rice, a meal
gomen nasai – I'm sorry, excuse me
gomibako – rubbish bin
gyōza – Chinese dumplings
gyūnyū – (cow's) milk

H
hairu – to enter, to sail (a ship)
hako – box
hama – beach
hana – flower
hanabi – fireworks
happyaku – eight hundred
hashi – chopsticks
hata – flags
hayai – fast, early
hayaku – early, quickly
hi – day, sun
hihīn – whinny
hikishio – current during low tide
hikkoshi suru – to relocate
hikōki – airplane
hikui – short, low
hirune suru – to have a nap
hito – person
hiyakedome – sunscreen
hō – way, side, alternative
hon – book
hosoi – small in diameter

I
ie – house
ii – good
ika – squid, cuttlefish
iku – to go
isu – chair
iu – to speak

J
jama – obstacle, hindrance
jitensha – bicycle
jugyō – lesson
jugyōchū – during the lesson
jūkyū – nineteen
junban – turn, order
jūsho – address

K
kabe – wall
kaeru – frog
kaidan – stairs, staircase
kakīn – the sound of a bat hitting a ball
kakkō – appearance
kakkoii – good appearance
kaku – to write, to draw
kamome – seagull
kasa – umbrella
kau – to buy
kawa – river
kaze – a cold
kaze o hiku – to catch a cold
kazoku – family
kikō – climate
kiku – to listen, to ask
kingyo – goldfish
ki o tsukeru – to be careful
kippu – ticket
kirei – pretty, clean
kodomo – child
koe – voice
koko – here
kokuban – blackboard
kokusai – international
korogaru – to roll
koro koro – the sound of something rolling
kotatsu – foot warmer
kotchi – this
kotoshi – this year
kū – to eat
kudasai – please
kūkō – airport
kuma – bear
kun – boy's honorific suffix
kuru – to come

kuruma – car
kusa – grass
kyō – today
kyōshitsu – classroom

M
mada – still, yet
made – until
mainichi – every day
mama – (suffix indicating state or condition)
matsu – to wait
megane – glasses
mimi – ear
minato – harbor
minna, mina – everybody
miru – to see
mizu – water
mizugi – swimwear
mo – too, as well
momo – peach
monosashi – ruler

N
na – (adjectival suffix)
nabe – saucepan
nagasaresō ni – almost washed away, almost dumped
naka – inside
naku – to cry, to crow, to chirp, to bleat, to croak, etc.
nami – waves
narasu – to pop, to click
naru – to become
natsu – summer
neko – cat
nezumi – mouse, rat
ni – in, at (destination indicator)
nichi – day
niwatori – chicken
no – of
nohara – field, meadow
nomu – to drink
nuru – to paint, to apply
nusumu – to steal

O
ōi – numerous, many
oishii – delicious
okāsan – mother
okashi – sweets, candy
okashii – funny, strange
ōkii – big, loud
okoru – to become angry
oku – to put, to place
okyakusan – guest, visitor or customer
onē-san – elder sister, girl
onna no ko – girl
oriru – to get off, to dismount
otoko no ko – boy
otōsan – father
oyogu – to swim

P
paka paka – clip clop

R
randoseru – knapsack, schoolbag
reizōko – refrigerator
renraku – contact
renshū – practice
rōka – corridor
ryokan – Japanese style inn
ryōri – cooking
ryōshūsho – receipt

S
sake – sake
sanpo – stroll
sara – plate, dish
sasu – to indicate, to point, to put up (an umbrella)
sayōnara – farewell

se – height, stature
seikaku – accuracy, character, nature
seito – student
sensei – teacher
shikaku – square
shinkansen – the bullet train
shinpai – worry, concern
shitsurei – rudeness
suiei – swimming
suimen – water surface
suki – to like, to love
sumu – to live
sunahama – the sands
sunayama – sandcastle
suru – to do
sushi – sushi, fish on vinegared rice
susono – foothills

T
tabemono – food
taberu – to eat
taikai – festival
taiko – drum
taisō – gymnastics
taiyō – sun
takai – tall, high, expensive
tanoshii – enjoyable, pleasurable
tataku – to beat, to hit
tatami – tatami, straw mat
tatsu – to stand, to rise
tegami – letter
tera – temple
tesuri – hand rail
tōi – far, distant, remote
tokei – clock
tokonoma – tokonoma, ornamental alcove
tokui – one's strong point
tomaru – to stop
tomodachi – friend
totemo – very, extremely
tsuchi – earth, soil, the ground
tsuitachi – the first of the month
tsukaikata – style of using
tsukau – to use
tsukue – desk
tsumetai – cold
tsuyoi – strong

U
ue – above, up, on
ugoku – to move
uma – horse
umareru – to be born
umi – the ocean
ureshii – happy
ushi – cow
utsu – to hit

W
wa – (subject indicator)
waruiko – naughty child
watashi – I, me

Y
yakyū – baseball
yakyūsenshu – baseball player
yama – mountain
yaoya – vegetable store
yasai – vegetables
yasashii – kind, gentle
yasumi – holiday, vacation
yoi – good
yoiko – good child
yomu – to read
yubi – finger, toe
yūhi – sunset
yukkuri – slowly
yūmei – famous